T0340141

About This Book

Why This Book Is Important

Costs and ROI: Evaluating at the Ultimate Level, the fifth book in the M&E series, discusses the ultimate level of evaluation: calculating ROI. Executives want to know whether specific programs and projects add value to their organization; calculating the ROI gives them the accountability they seek.

Part of calculating ROI is tabulating the fully loaded program costs. Fully loaded costs include all direct and indirect costs. Using fully loaded costs is critical in order to maintain a conservative approach.

What This Book Achieves

This book shows how to tabulate the fully loaded costs of a program and explains what costs should be included in this total. It also presents the different formulas that can be used to calculate ROI. Finally, measures other than ROI that can show the value of programs and projects are defined and explained.

How This Book Is Organized

This book begins with a brief introduction to the ROI process model and the Twelve Guiding Principles. Chapter One discusses why tabulating costs and calculating the ROI are important. It also examines why the ROI should be forecast. Chapter Two discusses how to efficiently track costs and explores the issues involved in cost tracking and cost categories. Cost reporting, cost accumulation, and cost estimation are also discussed.

Chapter Three details the calculation of ROI. The chapter includes examples as well as different ways to calculate the return and other measures. Chapter Four reviews the many concerns, issues, and myths surrounding the ROI Methodology.

In Chapter Five, the many benefits of developing an ROI forecast are discussed. Forecasts can be developed prior to a program's implementation by using a pilot program, reaction data, learning data, or skills and competencies. Finally, the guidelines for forecasting are examined.

The Measurement and Evaluation Series

Editors

Patricia Pulliam Phillips, Ph.D.

Jack J. Phillips, Ph.D.

Introduction to the Measurement and Evaluation Series

The ROI Six Pack provides detailed information on developing ROI evaluations, implementing the ROI Methodology, and showing the value of a variety of functions and processes. With detailed examples, tools, templates, shortcuts, and checklists, this series will be a valuable reference for individuals interested in using the ROI Methodology to show the impact of their projects, programs, and processes.

The Need

Although financial ROI has been measured for over one hundred years to quantify the value of plants, equipment, and companies, the concept has only recently been applied to evaluate the impact of learning and development, human resources, technology, quality, marketing, and other support functions. In the learning and development field alone, the use of ROI has become routine in many organizations. In the past decade, hundreds of organizations have embraced the ROI process to show the impact of many different projects and programs.

Along the way, professionals and practitioners need help. They need tools, templates, and tips, along with explanations, examples, and details, to make this process work. Without this help, using the ROI Methodology to show the value of projects and programs is difficult. In short, practitioners need shortcuts and proven techniques to minimize the resources required to use this process. Practitioners' needs have created the need for this series. This series will provide the detail necessary to make the ROI Methodology successful within an organization. For easy reference and use, the books are logically arranged to align with the steps of the ROI Methodology.

Audience

The principal audience for these books is individuals who plan to use the ROI Methodology to show the value of their projects and programs. Such individuals are specialists or managers charged with proving the value of their particular project or program. They need detailed information, know-how, and confidence.

A second audience is those who have used the ROI Methodology for some time but want a quick reference with tips and techniques to make ROI implementation more successful within their organization. This series, which explains the evaluation process in detail, will be a valuable reference set for these individuals, regardless of other ROI publications owned.

A third audience is consultants and researchers who want to know how to address specific evaluation issues. Three important challenges face individuals as they measure ROI and conduct ROI evaluations: (1) collecting post-program data, (2) isolating the effects of the program, and (3) converting data to monetary values. A book is devoted to each of these critical issues, allowing researchers and consultants to easily find details on each issue.

A fourth audience is those who are curious about the ROI Methodology and its use. The first book in this series focuses specifically on ROI, its use, and how to determine whether it is appropriate for an organization. When interest is piqued, the remaining books provide more detail.

Flow of the Books

The six books are presented in a logical sequence, mirroring the ROI process model. Book one, *ROI Fundamentals: Why and When to Measure ROI*, presents the basic ROI Methodology and makes the business case for measuring ROI as it explores the benefits and barriers to implementation. It also examines the type of organization best suited for the ROI Methodology and the best time to implement it. Planning for an ROI evaluation is also explored in this book.

Book two, *Data Collection: Planning For and Collecting All Types of Data*, details data collection by examining the different techniques, methods, and issues involved in this process, with an emphasis on collecting post-program data. It examines the different data collection methods: questionnaires, interviews, focus groups, observation, action plans, performance contracts, and monitoring records.

Book three, *Isolation of Results: Defining the Impact of the Program*, focuses on the most valuable part of the ROI Methodology and the essential step for ensuring credibility. Recognizing that factors other than the program being measured can influence results, this book shows a variety of ways in which the effects of a program can be isolated from other influences. Techniques include comparison analysis using a control group, trend line analysis and forecasting methods, and expert input from a variety of sources.

Book four, *Data Conversion: Calculating the Monetary Benefits*, covers perhaps the second toughest challenge of ROI evaluation: placing monetary value on program benefits. To calculate the ROI, data must be converted to money, and *Data Conversion* shows how this conversion has been accomplished in a variety of organizations. The good news is that standard values are available for many items. When they are not, the book shows different techniques for converting them, ranging from calculating the value from records to seeking experts and searching databases. When data cannot be converted to money credibly and with minimum resources, they are considered intangible. This book explores the range of intangible benefits and the necessary techniques for collecting, analyzing, and recording them.

Book five, *Costs and ROI: Evaluating at the Ultimate Level*, focuses on costs and ROI. This book shows that all costs must be captured in order to create a fully loaded cost profile. All the costs must be included in order to be conservative and to give the analysis additional credibility. Next, the actual ROI calculation is presented, showing the various assumptions and issues that must be addressed when calculating the ROI. Three different calculations are presented: the benefit-cost ratio, the ROI percentage, and the payback period. The book concludes with several cautions and concerns about the use of ROI and its meaning.

Book six, *Communication and Implementation: Sustaining the Practice*, explores two important issues. The first issue is reporting the results of an evaluation. This is the final part of the ROI Methodology and is necessary to ensure that audiences have the information they need so that improvement processes can be implemented. A range of techniques is available, including face-to-face meetings, brief reports, one-page summaries, routine communications, mass-audience techniques, and electronic media. All are available for reporting evaluation results. The final part of the book focuses on how to sustain the ROI evaluation process: how to use it, keep it going, and make it work in the long term to add value to the organization and, often, to show the value of all the programs and projects within a function or department.

Terminology: Programs, Projects, Solutions

In this series the terms *program* and *project* are used to describe many processes that can be evaluated using the ROI Methodology. This is an important issue because readers may vary widely in their perspectives. Individuals involved in technology applications may

Table I.1. Terms and Applications

Term	Example
Program	Leadership development skills enhancement for senior executives
Project	A reengineering scheme for a plastics division
System	A fully interconnected network for all branches of a bank
Initiative	A faith-based effort to reduce recidivism
Policy	A new preschool plan for disadvantaged citizens
Procedure	A new scheduling arrangement for truck drivers
Event	A golf outing for customers
Meeting	A U.S. Coast Guard conference on innovations
Process	Quality sampling
People	Staff additions in the customer care center
Tool	A new means of selecting hotel staff

use the terms *system* and *technology* rather than *program* or *project*. In public policy, in contrast, the word *program* is prominent. For a professional meetings and events planner, the word *program* may not be pertinent, but in human resources, *program* is often used. Finding one term for all these situations would be difficult. Consequently, the terms *program* and *project* are used interchangeably. Table I.1 lists these and other terms that may be used in other contexts.

Features

Each book in the series takes a straightforward approach to make it understandable, practical, and useful. Checklists are provided, charts are included, templates are presented, and examples are explored. All are intended to show how the ROI Methodology works. The focus of these books is implementing the process and making it successful within an organization. The methodology is based on the work of hundreds of individuals who have made the ROI Methodology a successful evaluation process within their organizations.

About Pfeiffer

Pfeiffer serves the professional development and hands-on resource needs of training and human resource practitioners and gives them products to do their jobs better. We deliver proven ideas and solutions from experts in HR development and HR management, and we offer effective and customizable tools to improve workplace performance. From novice to seasoned professional, Pfeiffer is the source you can trust to make yourself and your organization more successful.

Essential Knowledge Pfeiffer produces insightful, practical, and comprehensive materials on topics that matter the most to training and HR professionals. Our Essential Knowledge resources translate the expertise of seasoned professionals into practical, how-to guidance on critical workplace issues and problems. These resources are supported by case studies, worksheets, and job aids and are frequently supplemented with CD-ROMs, websites, and other means of making the content easier to read, understand, and use.

Essential Tools Pfeiffer's Essential Tools resources save time and expense by offering proven, ready-to-use materials–including exercises, activities, games, instruments, and assessments–for use during a training or team-learning event. These resources are frequently offered in looseleaf or CD-ROM format to facilitate copying and customization of the material.

Pfeiffer also recognizes the remarkable power of new technologies in expanding the reach and effectiveness of training. While e-hype has often created whizbang solutions in search of a problem, we are dedicated to bringing convenience and enhancements to proven training solutions. All our e-tools comply with rigorous functionality standards. The most appropriate technology wrapped around essential content yields the perfect solution for today's on-the-go trainers and human resource professionals.

Pfeiffer *Essential resources for training and HR professionals*
www.pfeiffer.com

Costs and ROI

Evaluating
at the Ultimate Level

Jack J. Phillips, Ph.D.
Lizette Zúñiga, M.A.

Pfeiffer

A Wiley Imprint
www.pfeiffer.com

Published by Pfeiffer
An Imprint of Wiley
989 Market Street, San Francisco, CA 94103-1741
www.pfeiffer.com

Wiley Bicentennial logo: Richard J. Pacifico

For additional copies/bulk purchases of this book in the U.S. please contact 800-274-4434.

Pfeiffer books and products are available through most bookstores. To contact Pfeiffer directly call our Customer Care Department within the U.S. at 800-274-4434, outside the U.S. at 317-572-3985, fax 317-572-4002, or visit www.pfeiffer.com.

Pfeiffer also publishes its books in a variety of electronic formats. Some content that appears in print may not be available in electronic books.

Library of Congress Cataloging-in-Publication Data

Phillips, Jack J., date.
    Costs and ROI: evaluating at the ultimate level/Jack J. Phillips, Lizette Zúñiga.
      p. cm.
    Includes bibliographical references and index.
    ISBN: 978-0-7879-8721-3 (pbk.)
    1. Employees—Training of—Cost effectiveness.   2. Employees—Training of—Evaluation.   3. Personnel management—Evaluation.   4. Rate of return—Evaluation.
I. Zúñiga, Lizette.   II. Title.
    HF5549.5.T7P427   2008
    658.3'124—dc22
                                                                        2007045001

Production Editor: Michael Kay   Editorial Assistant: Julie Rodriguez
Editor: Matthew Davis   Manufacturing Supervisor: Becky Morgan
Printed in the United States of America
PB Printing 10 9 8 7 6 5 4 3 2 1

Contents

Chapter 5: ROI Forecasting — 103

Acknowledgments from the Editors

From Patti

No project, regardless of its size or scope, is completed without the help and support of others. My sincere thanks go to the staff at Pfeiffer. Their support for this project has been relentless. Matt Davis has been the greatest! It is our pleasure and privilege to work with such a professional and creative group of people.

Thanks also go to my husband, Jack. His unwavering support of my work is always evident. His idea for the series was to provide readers with a practical understanding of the various components of a comprehensive measurement and evaluation process. Thank you, Jack, for another fun opportunity!

From Jack

Many thanks go to the staff who helped make this series a reality. Lori Ditoro did an excellent job of meeting a very tight deadline and delivering a quality manuscript.

Much admiration and thanks go to Patti. She is an astute observer of the ROI Methodology, having observed and learned from hundreds of presentations, consulting assignments, and engagements. In addition, she is an excellent researcher and student of the process, studying how it is developed and how it works. She has become an ROI expert in her own right. Thanks, Patti, for your many contributions. You are a great partner, friend, and spouse.

Principles of the ROI Methodology

The ROI Methodology is a step-by-step tool for evaluating any program, project, or initiative in any organization. Figure P.1 illustrates the ROI process model, which makes a potentially complicated process simple by breaking it into sequential steps. The ROI process model provides a systematic, step-by-step approach to ROI evaluations that helps keep the process manageable, allowing users to address one issue at a time. The model also emphasizes that the ROI Methodology is a logical, systematic process that flows from one step to another and provides a way for evaluators to collect and analyze six types of data.

Applying the model consistently from one program to another is essential for successful evaluation. To aid consistent application of the model, the ROI Methodology is based on twelve Guiding Principles. These principles are necessary for a credible, conservative approach to evaluation through the different levels.

1. When conducting a higher-level evaluation, collect data at lower levels.

2. When planning a higher-level evaluation, the previous level of evaluation is not required to be comprehensive.

3. When collecting and analyzing data, use only the most credible sources.

Figure P.1. The ROI Process Model

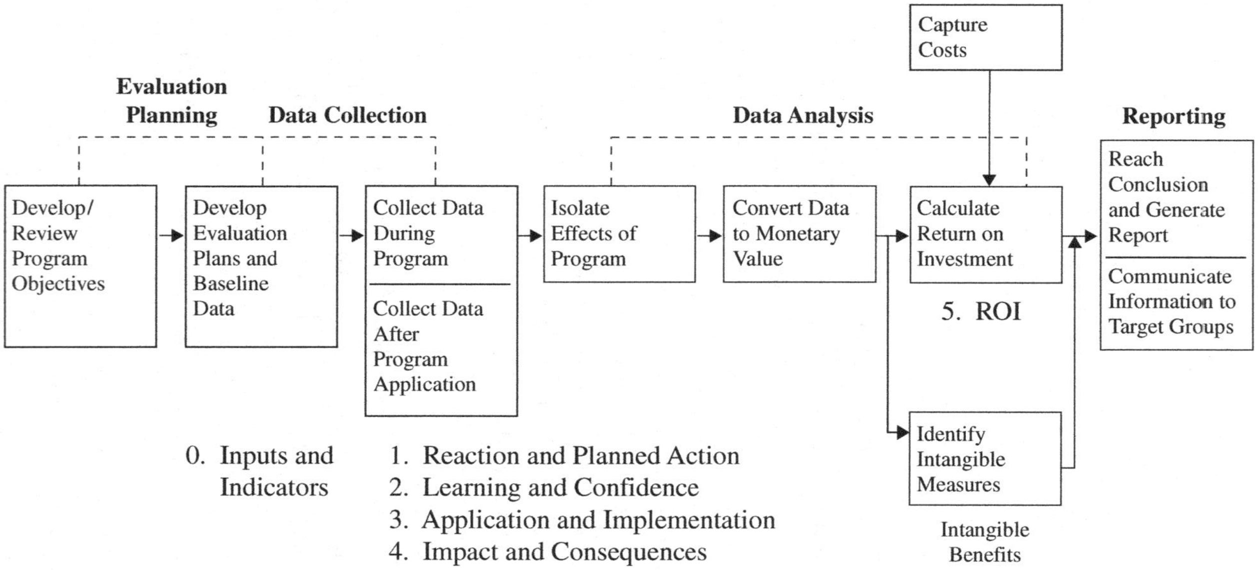

| Evaluation Planning | Data Collection | | Data Analysis | | | Reporting |

4. When analyzing data, select the most conservative alternative for calculations.

5. Use at least one method to isolate the effects of a project.

6. If no improvement data are available for a population or from a specific source, assume that little or no improvement has occurred.

7. Adjust estimates of improvement for potential errors of estimation.

8. Avoid use of extreme data items and unsupported claims when calculating ROI.

9. Use only the first year of annual benefits in ROI analysis of short-term solutions.

10. Fully load all costs of a solution, project, or program when analyzing ROI.

11. Intangible measures are defined as measures that are purposely not converted to monetary values.

12. Communicate the results of the ROI Methodology to all key stakeholders.

1

The Importance of Costs and ROI

The costs of programs and projects are increasing, creating more pressure on managers to know how and why money is spent. Sometimes, the total cost of a program is required, which means that the cost profile must go beyond the direct costs to include all indirect costs as well. Cost information is used to manage resources, develop standards, measure efficiencies, and examine alternative delivery processes.

Tabulating program costs is an essential step in calculating ROI; program costs are the denominator in the ROI formula. Thus, it is just as important to focus on costs as it is to focus on benefits. In practice, costs are often more easily captured than benefits. This chapter explores the costs accumulation and tabulation steps, outlines the specific costs that should be captured, and presents economical ways to develop costs.

When ROI calculations are developed, understanding the alternatives to the ROI calculation and their relationship to each other is important. In addition, it is necessary to know what ROI means and how it should be used in an organization. This book shows how costs and ROI calculations are developed and how the ROI Methodology can be used as a forecasting tool. This opening chapter outlines the importance of tracking and monitoring costs, developing the ROI, and forecasting.

Why Be Concerned About Costs?

Apart from the fact that cost figures are required for the ROI calculation, costs should be tracked and monitored for many reasons. Today's organizations focus on understanding and controlling costs; having an appropriate framework for keeping track of costs and using them in different ways allows a department or organization to be more efficient—an important advantage in a globally competitive market.

Benchmarking

Many factors have contributed to the increased attention now given to monitoring costs accurately and thoroughly. Every organization must know how much money it spends on programs and projects and functions. Many organizations calculate these expenditures and compare the amounts with those of other organizations, although comparisons are difficult to make because organizations often have different bases for cost calculations. For example, some organizations calculate learning and development costs as a percentage of payroll costs and set targets for increased investment. In the United States, the average is about 2 percent, whereas in Europe it is 3 percent, and in Asia and Latin America it is 3.8 percent. The benchmarks are often the basis for developing financial allocation.

An effective system of cost monitoring enables an organization to calculate the magnitude of total expenditures. Collecting this information also helps management answer two important questions:

- How much do we spend on our function compared with other functions?

- How much should we be spending?

Exhibit 1.1 presents an exercise that may be helpful in addressing these two questions. The table focuses on setting a spending

Exhibit 1.1. Setting Spending Amounts: How Much Should You Spend on Human Resources?

Overall Expenditures	Your Estimate	Actual	Target
Total expenditures for human resources[1]			
Total expenditures for human capital[2]			
Spending on human resources as a percentage of payroll			
Spending on human resources as a percentage of revenues			
Spending on human resources as a percentage of operating costs			
Spending on human resources per employee			

Functional Area	Your Estimate (percentage)	Actual (percentage)	Target (percentage)
Needs assessment			
Development			
Delivery and implementation			
Operations, maintenance			
Evaluation			
Total	**100%**	**100%**	**100%**

(Continued)

Exhibit 1.1. Setting Spending Amounts: How Much Should You Spend on Human Resources? (*Continued*)

Questions for Discussion

1. Is there a significant difference between estimated and actual costs?

   ☐ Yes   ☐ No

   Explain: _____

   _____

2. How did you determine what your targets would be?

   _____

   _____

3. What should you spend?

   _____

   _____

[1]Total expenditures for human resources = all costs associated with human resources (for example, recruitment, selection, development, compensation).

[2]Total expenditures for human capital = total expenditures for human resources plus the total salaries and benefits of all employees.

amount for the human resources function. The human resources manager could compare actual expenditures with those of organizations considered best practice.

Although this exercise focuses on setting the value for human resources spending, it can be adapted for any function—for example, learning and development, meetings and events, technology, or quality. In the first part of the exercise, estimate the expenditures in each of the areas. Make rough estimates, without making any calculations or searching for the data. Then fill in the actual expenditure in each area if it can easily be found or developed. If estimates must be developed, use a more reliable value than the initial estimate, including input from other individuals. Next, set a target for the expenditure, based on a desire to follow best practices, to overcome gaps in current spending levels, or to pursue other specific goals. Overall expenditures represent expenditures as they relate to organizational funding. Functional area expenditures are those for specific programming functions. The remainder of the exercise consists of questions that reflect on the issues in the exercise.

This exercise focuses on the process of setting spending levels, which are not clearly defined and are not given enough attention in many organizations. Although total spending levels are set by budgets, the process of arriving at those values is sometimes less comprehensive and less thought out than is desirable.

Evaluation

The staff of any functional area should know the relative cost-effectiveness of their programs and the components of those programs. Monitoring costs by program allows the staff to evaluate the relative contribution of a program and determine how those costs are changing. If a program's cost rises, it might be appropriate to reevaluate the program's impact and overall success. Comparing specific cost components with those of other programs or organizations may be useful. For example, the cost per participant for one program could be compared with the cost per participant for a similar program. A huge difference may indicate a problem. Also, costs associated with design, development, or delivery of a program could be compared with those costs for other programs within the organization and used to develop cost standards.

When a return on investment or cost benefit analysis is needed for a specific program, costs must be developed. One of the most significant reasons for collecting costs is to obtain data for use in a benefit-cost comparison. In this comparison, cost data are as important as the program's economic benefits.

Cost Forecasting

Accurate costs are necessary in order to predict future costs. Historical costs for a program provide the basis for predicting future costs of a similar program or budgeting for a program. When an ROI forecast is needed, predicted costs must be developed. Sophisticated cost models make it possible to estimate or predict costs with reasonable accuracy.

Efficiency

Controlling costs is necessary in order to improve the efficiency of a functional area. Competitive pressures place increased attention on the need for efficiencies. Most departments have monthly budgets with cost projections listed by various accounts and, in some cases, by program. Cost monitoring is an excellent tool for identifying problem areas and taking corrective action. From a mere management standpoint, accumulation of cost data is a necessity.

Other Reasons for Monitoring Costs

Exhibit 1.2 summarizes why costs should be developed. As this list illustrates, there are many reasons why capturing costs is necessary, beyond calculating ROI.

Exhibit 1.2. Why Develop Costs?

- To determine overall expenditures

- To determine the relative cost of individual programs

- To predict future program costs

- To calculate benefits versus costs for a specific program

- To improve the efficiency of a department

- To evaluate alternatives to a proposed program

- To plan and budget for next year's operation

- To develop a marginal cost pricing system

- To integrate data into other systems

The Importance of ROI

"Show me the money." There's nothing new about this statement, especially in business. Organizations of all types want to see the money – specifically they want to see a return on their investments. What's new is the method that organizations can use to get there. While "showing the money" is the ultimate report of value, organization leaders recognize that value lies in the eye of the beholder; therefore, the method used to show the money must also show the value as it is perceived by all stakeholders. Just as important, organizations need a methodology that provides data to help improve investment decisions. This book presents an approach that does both: it assesses the value that organizations receive for investing in programs and projects, and it develops data to improve those programs by providing all stakeholders with the information they need to make decisions. These decisions will drive change, improvement, and ultimately value for the organization.

The Ultimate Level of Evaluation

ROI represents the newest way to state value. In the past, the success of a program, project, or process was measured by activity: number of people involved, money spent, days to complete. For example, Motorola measured success by ensuring that every employee must complete forty hours of learning annually. Other companies also used forty hours of learning as a benchmark of success. While utilization metrics describe the level of activity and consumption, these measures do not define value. Little consideration is given to the benefits derived from the activity. Value is defined by results, not activity. More frequently than ever before, value is defined as monetary benefits compared with costs: ROI. ROI is the ultimate level of evaluation. The following examples illustrate this point.

- The U.S. Air Force developed the ROI for an information assurance program to prevent intrusion into its computer databases.

- Apple calculated the ROI for its process improvement teams.

- Sprint/NEXTEL computed the ROI on its diversity program.

- The Australian Capital Territory Community Care agency forecast the ROI for the implementation of a client relationship management system.

- Accenture calculated the ROI on a new sales platform for its consultants.

- Wachovia developed an ROI forecast and then measured the actual ROI for its negotiations program.

- A major hotel chain calculated the financial value and ROI of its coaching program.

- The cities of New York, San Francisco, and Phoenix showed the monetary value of investing in programs to reduce the number of homeless citizens on the streets.

- Cisco Systems is measuring the ROI for its key meetings and events.

- A major U.S. Defense Department agency calculated the ROI for a master's degree program offered by a major university.

Although the ROI Methodology had its beginnings in the 1970s, it has expanded in recent years to become the most comprehensive and far-reaching approach to demonstrating the value of program investment.

Types of Values

Value is determined by stakeholders' perspectives, which may include organizational, spiritual, personal, and social values. Value is defined by consumers, taxpayers, and shareholders in many different ways. Capitalism defines value as the economic contribution to shareholders. The global reporting initiative, established in 1997, defines value from three perspectives: environmental, economic, and societal.

Even as projects, processes, and programs are implemented to improve the social, environmental, and economic climates, their monetary value is often sought in order to ensure that resources are allocated appropriately and that investments reap a return. No longer is it enough to report the number of programs offered, the number of participants or volunteers trained, or the dollars generated through a fundraising effort. Stakeholders at all levels—including executives, shareholders, managers and supervisors, taxpayers, project designers, and participants—are looking for outcomes—improvement in output, quality, costs, and time—and in many cases they want a specific outcome: the ROI.

ROI Is King

Some people are concerned that too much focus is placed on economic value, but it is economics, or money, that allows organizations and individuals to contribute to the greater good. Monetary resources are limited; they can be put to best use, or they can be underused or overused. In the French language, *roi* is the word for king, and ROI is indeed king, for determining ROI is the best way for organizations to show that their programs deliver monetary value to the organization. Organizations and individuals have choices about where they invest their resources. To ensure that monetary resources are put to best use, they must be allocated to the programs, processes, and projects that yield the greatest return.

For example, if a process improvement initiative is designed to improve efficiencies and it subsequently does improve efficiencies, one might assume that the initiative was successful. But if the initiative cost more than the efficiency gains are worth, has value been added to the organization? Could a less expensive process have yielded similar or even better results, possibly reaping a positive ROI? Questions like these should be asked on a routine basis. No longer will activity suffice as a measure of program results. A new generation of decision makers is defining value in a new way, by measuring programs' impact on business performance.

The "Show Me" Generation

Figure 1.1 illustrates the requirements of the new "show me" generation. "Show me" implies that stakeholders want to see actual data (that is, numbers and measures). This impulse accounted for the initial attempt to see value in programs. This evolved into "show me the money," a direct call for financial results. But financial results alone do not provide the evidence needed to ensure that programs add value. Often, a connection between programs and value is assumed, but that assumption soon must give way to the need to show an actual connection by isolating the effects of the program from other influences. Hence, "show me the real money" was an

Figure 1.1. The Evolution of "Show Me"

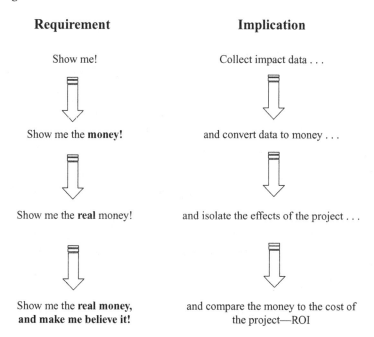

Requirement	Implication
Show me!	Collect impact data . . .
Show me the **money!**	and convert data to money . . .
Show me the **real** money!	and isolate the effects of the project . . .
Show me the **real money, and make me believe it!**	and compare the money to the cost of the project—ROI

attempt at establishing credibility. This phase, though critical, still left stakeholders with an unanswered question: "Do the monetary benefits linked to the program outweigh the costs?" This question is the mantra for the new "show me" generation: "Show me the real money, and make me believe it." This demand is answered by measuring ROI. But this new generation of program sponsors also recognizes that value is more than just a single number: value is what motivates the entire organization. Hence, the need to report value based on the definitions of various people throughout the organization has arisen.

The New Definition of Value

The changing perspectives on value and the shifts that are occurring in organizations have all led to a new definition of value. Value is not defined as a single number. Rather, value is defined by a variety of data points. Value must be balanced with quantitative and qualitative data, as well as financial and nonfinancial data. The data sometimes reflect tactical issues, such as activity, as well as strategic issues, such as ROI. Value must be derived from different time frames and not necessarily represent a single point in time. It must reflect the value systems that are important to stakeholders. The data that are used to assess value must be collected from credible sources, using cost-effective methods; and value must be action-oriented, compelling individuals to make adjustments and changes.

The processes used to calculate ROI must be consistent from one program to another. Standards must be in place so that results can be compared. These standards must support conservative outcomes, leaving broader assumptions to decision makers. The ROI Methodology presented in this book meets all the preceding criteria for assessing value. The ROI Methodology generates six types of data that address the issues raised by the new definition of value: reaction and perceived value, learning and confidence, application and implementation, impact and consequences, return on investment, and intangible benefits.

Why ROI Now?

In recent years, a variety of forces have driven additional focus on measuring the impact of programs, including the financial contribution and ROI. These forces have challenged old ways of defining program success.

Program Failures

Almost every organization has undertaken unsuccessful programs—programs that go astray, costing far too much and failing to deliver on promises. Program disasters occur in business organizations and in government and nonprofit organizations. Some program disasters are legendary. Some are swept into closets or covered up, but they are there, and their numbers are far too large to tolerate (Nickson and Siddons, 2005). The large number of failures has generated increased concerns about measuring project and program success before, during, and after implementation. Many critics suggest that program failure might be avoided more often if (1) programs are based on a legitimate need; (2) adequate planning is in place at the outset; (3) data are collected throughout the program to confirm that the implementation is on track; (4) an impact study is conducted to detail the program's contribution; and (5) the program's monetary benefits are compared to the program's costs (in other words, ROI is calculated). Unfortunately, sometimes these steps are unintentionally omitted, are not fully understood, or are purposely ignored; to counteract these tendencies, greater emphasis is being placed on processes of accountability. This book shows how these five elements can come together to create value-adding projects and programs.

Increased Total Program Costs

As the costs of programs and projects continue to rise, their budgets become targets for others who would like to have that money for their own programs. What was once considered a mere cost of doing business is now considered an investment that must be wisely allocated. For example, consider the field of learning and development in the United States. Of course, learning and development programs are necessary in order to introduce new skills and technology to employees, but twenty years ago they were regarded by some company executives as a frivolous expense. These days, the annual direct cost of organizational learning and development is estimated to be over $100 billion in the United States. A few large organizations spend as much as $1 billion every year on corporate learning and development. With numbers like these, learning and development is no longer considered a frivolous expense; rather, it is regarded as an investment, and many executives expect a return on that investment.

Trend Toward Greater Accountability

A consistent and persistent trend in accountability is evident in organizations across the globe: almost every function, process, program, or initiative is judged against higher standards than in the past. Various functions in organizations are attempting to show their worth by capturing and demonstrating the value they add to the organization. They compete for funds; therefore, they have to show value, including ROI. For example, in many organizations, the research and development function must show its value in monetary terms in order to compete with mainstream processes such as sales and production, which have been showing their value in direct monetary terms for more than a century.

Staff Support Managers' New Business Focus

In the past, managers of many support functions in government, nonprofit, and private-sector organizations had no business experience. Today, things have changed; many managers of support functions have a business background, a formal business education, or a business focus. These managers are more aware of bottom-line issues in their organization and are more knowledgeable about operational and financial concerns. They often take a business approach to their processes, and evaluating ROI is a part of that strategy. Because of their background, they are familiar with the concept of ROI. They have used ROI calculations in their academic studies to evaluate decisions to purchase equipment, build new facilities, or buy a company. As a result, they understand and appreciate the applications of ROI and are eager to apply it in their own operations.

Support functions are often regarded as overhead, a burden on the organization, and an unnecessary expense. These days, the approach of many managers is to outsource, automate, or eliminate overhead operations. Great strides have been made in all three approaches. Consequently, staff support departments must prove their value in order to be accepted as viable support functions or administrative processes, and this proof often includes ROI calculations on major programs.

Evidence-Based or Fact-Based Management

In recent years, there has been an important trend toward fact-based or evidence-based management. Traditionally, many key decisions were based on instinct and gut feelings; now, more managers are using sophisticated, detailed processes to show the value of their projects and programs. Quality decisions must be based on more than gut feelings experienced in the blink of an eye. With a comprehensive set of measures, including financial ROI, better organizational decisions about people, products, programs, and processes are possible.

When taken seriously, evidence-based management can change how a manager thinks and acts. It is a way of seeing the world and thinking about the craft of management. Evidence-based management proceeds from the premise that using better, deeper logic and facts to the extent possible helps leaders do their jobs better. It is based on the belief that facing the hard facts about what works and what doesn't work and understanding and rejecting the total nonsense that often passes for sound advice will help organizations perform better (Pfeffer and Sutton, 2006). Moving to fact-based management makes it easier to expand performance measurement to include ROI calculations.

Limitations of Benchmarking

Many managers have been obsessed with benchmarking, using it to compare every type of process, function, and activity. Unfortunately, benchmarking has its limitations. First, best practices are sometimes elusive. Not all participants in a benchmarking program or report necessarily employ the best practices. In fact, just the opposite may be true: many benchmarking studies are developed by organizations that are willing to pay to participate. Second, what is needed by one organization is not always needed by another. A specific benchmarked measure or process may be of limited use in actual practice. Finally, benchmarking data are often devoid of financial information, reflecting few measures of actual financial contributions. Therefore, many managers are now asking for more specific internal processes that can evaluate those important financial measures.

Executive Appetite for Evaluation of ROI

Evaluation of monetary contribution and ROI is receiving increased interest in the executive suite. Top managers who have watched budgets continue to grow without the implementation of appropriate accountability measures are frustrated, and they are responding to the situation by turning to ROI assessment. Top executives now demand ROI calculations and proof of monetary contributions from departments and functions that previously were not required to provide them. For years, function managers and department heads convinced executives that their processes could not be measured and that the value of their activities should be taken at face value. Executives no longer buy that argument; they demand the same accountability from these functions as they do from the sales and production units of the organization. Such demands for accountability require organizations to shift their measurement processes to include the evaluation of financial impact and ROI.

Why Forecast ROI?

Although ROI calculations based on post-program data are the most accurate, sometimes it is important to forecast ROI before a program is initiated or before final results are tabulated. Several critical issues drive the need for a forecast before a program is completed or perhaps even before a program is pursued.

Expensive Programs and Projects

Because forecasting reduces uncertainty, it may be especially appropriate for costly programs. In these cases, implementation is not practical until the program has been analyzed to determine the potential ROI. For example, if a program involves a significant amount of effort in design, development, and implementation, a client may not even want to expend the resources for a pilot test unless some assurance of a positive ROI can be given. In another example, an expensive equipment purchase may be needed in order to launch a program. It may be necessary to forecast ROI prior to making the purchase, to ensure that the monetary value of the process outcomes outweighs the costs of equipment and implementation.

While there may be trade-offs in deploying a lower-profile, lower-cost pilot, the pre-program ROI is still important, prompting some clients to stand firm until an ROI forecast is produced.

High Risks and Uncertainty

Sponsors want to remove as much uncertainty as possible from the program and act on the best data available. This concern sometimes pushes the program team to forecast ROI before any resources are expended to design and implement the program. Some programs are high-risk opportunities or solutions. In addition to being expensive, they may represent critical initiatives that can make or break an organization. Or the situation may be one in which failure would be disastrous and there is only one chance to get it right. In these cases, the decision maker must have the best possible data, and the best possible data often include an ROI forecast.

For example, one large restaurant chain developed an unfortunate reputation for racial insensitivity and discrimination. The fallout brought many lawsuits and caused a public relations nightmare. The company undertook a major program to transform the organization, changing its image, attitudes, and actions. Because of the program's high stakes and critical nature, company executives requested a forecast before pursuing the program. They needed to know not only whether this major program would be worthwhile financially but also what specifically would change and how specifically the program would unfold. This analysis required a comprehensive forecast involving various levels of data, including the ROI.

Post-Program Comparison

An important reason for forecasting ROI is to see how well the forecast holds up under the scrutiny of post-program analysis. Whenever a plan is in place to collect data on a program's success, comparing actual results with pre-program expectations is helpful. In an ideal world, a forecast ROI would have a defined relationship with the actual ROI, or, at least, one would lead to the other, after adjustments. The forecast is often an inexpensive process because it involves estimates and assumptions. If the forecast becomes a reliable predictor of the post-program analysis, then the forecast ROI might substitute for the actual ROI. This could save money on post-program analysis.

Compliance

More than ever, organizations are requiring a forecast ROI before they undertake major programs. For example, one organization requires any program with a budget exceeding $500,000 to have a forecast ROI before it can receive program approval. Some units of government have enacted legislation that requires program forecasts. With increasing frequency, formal policy and legal structures are reasons for developing ROI forecasts. All of these reasons are leading more organizations to develop ROI forecasts so that their sponsors will have an estimate of programs' expected payoff.

Final Thoughts

This brief introductory chapter describes the rationale for tackling the key issues in this book. It shows why costs must be developed and reported on a routine basis for reasons other than the ROI calculation. This chapter also discusses the importance of measuring ROI and why ROI is evolving into a principal measurement requirement. In addition, this chapter explains when it is important to look into the future and forecast the ROI of a program before it is initiated. The next chapters will amplify these areas in much more detail.

References

Nickson, D., and Siddons, S. *Project Disasters and How to Survive Them*. London: Kogan Page, 2005.

Pfeffer, J., and Sutton, R. *Hard Facts, Dangerous Half-Truths and Total Nonsense: Profiting from Evidence-Based Management*. Boston: Harvard Business School Press, 2006.

2

Cost Tracking and Classification

Capturing costs is challenging because the figures must be accurate, reliable, and realistic. Although most organizations can calculate costs much more easily than they can calculate the economic value of benefits, the true cost of a program is often an elusive figure, even in some of the best organizations. While the total direct budget of a program can usually be easily obtained, determining all of the costs of a program, including the indirect costs related to it, is more difficult. In order for evaluators to calculate a realistic ROI, costs must be accurate and credible; otherwise, painstaking attention to evaluating the benefits will be wasted.

Cost Issues

Before we describe the ways to monitor and classify costs, it will be helpful to discuss a few important cost issues that affect the ways in which costs are tracked and classified.

Pressure to Disclose All Costs

The pressure to report all the costs of a program (the fully loaded costs) has increased. This takes the cost profile beyond the direct cost of the program to include the cost of the time that participants are involved in the program, including the benefits they earn during that time, as well as other overhead costs. For years, senior managers have realized that programs involve many indirect costs. Now, they are asking for an accounting for these costs.

The impact of indirect costs is illustrated by a situation in which management's control of a large state agency was being audited. A portion of the audit focused on training costs. The following comments are based on the auditor's report (ROI Institute, 2005, p. 37). Costs tracked at the program level focused on direct costs ("hard" costs) and ignored the cost of time that employees spent on preparing for, participating in, or supporting the training. For one program, including these costs raised the total training cost dramatically. The agency stated that the total two-year cost for the program was about $600,000. This figure included only direct costs and therefore was substantially low because it did not include the cost of the time spent by staff in preparing for and attending the program. The figure for time spent in preparatory work and attendance came to $1.39 million. When the statewide average of 45.5 percent for benefits was considered, the total indirect cost of staff time spent to prepare for and attend the program was more than $2 million. Finally, when the agency's direct costs of $600,000 were added to the more than $2 million indirect cost just noted, the total was more than $2.6 million. Among other factors that would drive actual costs higher still were the following:

- Cost of travel, meals, and lodging for participants in the training

- Allocated salaries and benefits of staff members who provided administrative and logistic support to the program

- Opportunity costs of productivity lost by staff in doing preparatory work and attending training

Failure to consider all indirect costs ("soft" costs) could have caused the agency to be out of compliance with the Fair Labor

Standards Act (FLSA), particularly as training filtered down to rank-and-file staff. Because FLSA requires that such staff be directly compensated for overtime, it would not be appropriate for the agency to ask such employees to complete preparatory work for the training sessions on their own time. Continuing to handle such overtime work in this way might also encourage false overtime reporting and skew overtime data through incorrect reporting, as well as increase the amount of uncompensated overtime.

Numerous barriers hampered agency efforts to determine "how much training costs."

- Cost systems tended to hide administrative, support, internal, and other indirect or soft costs.

- Costs generally were monitored at the division level rather than at the level of individual programs or activities.

- Cost information required by activity-based cost systems was not being generated.

As this case vividly demonstrates, the cost of training is much more than direct expenditures, and it is important that learning and development departments be expected to report fully loaded costs in their reports.

Fully Loaded Costs as a Conservative Approach

The conservative approach to calculating ROI encourages a specific approach to cost accumulation. Guiding Principle 10 states, "Fully load all costs of a solution, project, or program when analyzing ROI."

In this approach, all costs that can be identified and linked to a particular program are included. The rule is simple: in the denominator of the ROI formula, when in doubt, put it in. (That is, if it is questionable whether a cost should be included, it is recommended that it be included, even if the cost guidelines for an organization do not require it.). This parallels a rule for the numerator of the ROI formula, which states, "When in doubt, leave it out." (That is, if it is questionable whether a benefit should be included, it should be omitted from the ROI analysis.) When an ROI is calculated and reported to target audiences, the accuracy and credibility of the process should be capable of withstanding even the closest scrutiny. The only way to meet this test is to ensure that all costs are included. Of course, from a realistic viewpoint, if the controller or chief financial officer insists on not using certain costs, then it is best to leave them out.

Many professionals ask, "Why include items such as salaries of participants and in-house training and meeting facilities when reporting costs?" They rationalize that salaries are paid and in-house facility costs would be incurred even if the program were not implemented. Also, some would argue that the initial costs of analysis, design, and development should not be included because they represent "sunk" costs. Perhaps the most compelling reason to account for salaries, facilities, and other indirect cost items is that if they are not included, then the ROI will likely be overstated. An example of contrasting approaches is presented in Table 2.1. This table shows the data for a two-day program on negotiation skills, a one-time offering that included all thirty-six professional employees reporting to a manager (the client). The program was delivered by a supplier, using the supplier's materials and process. The annualized monetary benefit of the thirty-six participants' use of their improved skills was $240,000. Table 2.1 shows two approaches to calculating the costs of the program, one used by the program manager (Approach A) and one used by the client (Approach B).

The ROI calculations using both cost scenarios are shown here. ROI using Approach A cost tabulation:

$$\text{ROI} (\%) = \frac{\$240,000 - \$111,109}{\$111,109} \times 100 = 116\%$$

Table 2.1. Comparison of Cost Scenarios for a Negotiation Skills Program

Cost Item	Approach A: Tabulation of Fully Loaded Costs	Approach B: Tabulation of Direct Costs
Needs assessment (one-time cost)	$12,000	_____
Design and development (minimal redesign required to revise role-playing scenarios)	$2,000	_____
Delivery		
• Facilitator and coaching fees	$38,000	$38,000
• Travel expenses, facilitator	$2,900	$2,900
• Materials	$5,000	$5,000
• Refreshments	$900	$900
• Salaries and benefits, coordinator	$317	$317
• Travel expenses, coordinator	$700	$700
• Salaries and benefits, participants	$33,413	_____
• Travel expenses, participants	$3,600	$3,600
• In-house training facility and audiovisual equipment costs	$1,100	_____
Evaluation (one-time cost)	$9,000	$9,000
Overhead (2% of total program cost)	$2,179	$1,208
Total	$111,109	$61,625

Note: Annualized value of benefits from participation of thirty-six employees, after isolation of program effects, is $240,000.

ROI using Approach B cost tabulation:

$$\text{ROI (\%)} = \frac{\$240,000 - \$61,625}{\$61,625} \times 100 = 289\%$$

Approach B, which did not include participant salaries, the cost of in-house facilities, or the cost of the initial analysis and design, yielded an ROI that was more than twice that yielded by Approach A, which was fully loaded. The ROI was significantly overstated in Approach B.

Executives frequently review salaries and benefits in connection with other organizational costs. For example, when a request is made to hire additional staff, the central issue is how to justify spending the additional resources (that is, how will incurring this new cost benefit the organization?). The prospective expenditure for staff is analyzed in terms of "loaded cost," or the cost of one FTE (full-time equivalent). Even the expenses that will likely be incurred by the new employee are detailed as a separate item, increasing the benefit required to justify the hire. Executives are accustomed to using "all costs," direct and indirect. Anything short of this would be viewed as inadequate accounting.

The Danger of Accumulating Costs Without Tracking Benefits

Communicating the costs of a program without presenting benefits can be dangerous. Unfortunately, many organizations have fallen into this trap for years. Costs are presented to management in all types of ingenious ways, such as the cost of the program or the cost per employee. While these costs may be helpful for efficiency comparisons, presenting them without also presenting the benefits of a program may not be a good idea. When most executives review costs, they logically ask, "What benefit was received from this program?" This is a typical management reaction, particularly when costs seem too high. In deference to this logic, some organizations have adopted a policy of not communicating cost data for a program unless the benefits can be captured and presented along with the costs. Even if the benefit data are subjective and intangible, they are included with the cost data. This practice helps maintain a balanced perspective that examines both costs and benefits.

Policies and Guidelines

An organization's philosophy and policy on costs should be detailed in guidelines for staff members and others who monitor and report costs. Cost guidelines specify which costs should be included and how cost data should be captured, analyzed, and reported.

Cost guidelines can range from a one-page document to a fifty-page manual. The simpler approach is better. When fully developed, cost guidelines should be reviewed by the organization's finance and accounting staff. The final document serves as the guiding force for collecting, monitoring, and reporting costs. When ROI is calculated and reported, the costs are included in a summary and the cost guidelines are referenced in a footnote or attached as an appendix.

Cost Tracking Issues

We will now discuss how costs are collected and classified within organizations.

Sources of Program Costs

The three major sources of program costs are illustrated in Table 2.2. Staff expenses usually represent the greatest portion of costs and are sometimes transferred directly to the client or program sponsor. The second major cost category consists of participant expenses, both direct and indirect. These costs are not identified in

Table 2.2. Sources of Program Costs

Source of Costs	Cost Reporting Issues
Staff expenses	• Costs are usually accurate. • Variable expenses may be underestimated.
Participant expenses (direct and indirect)	• Direct expenses are usually not fully loaded. • Indirect expenses are rarely included in program costs.
External expenses (equipment and services)	• External expenses are sometimes understated. • It may be difficult to hold external vendors accountable for their expenditures.

many programs; nevertheless, they represent a significant amount. The third source of program costs is payments made to external resources, including payments to hotels and conference centers, equipment suppliers, and providers of services prescribed in the program. As Table 2.2 shows, many of the costs in these categories are often understated. Financial and accounting systems should be able to track and report the costs from these sources. The process presented in this book is capable of tracking these costs, too.

Process Steps and Costs

Another important way to consider costs is in the context of how a program unfolds. Figure 2.1 shows the typical program cycle,

Figure 2.1. Program Cycle

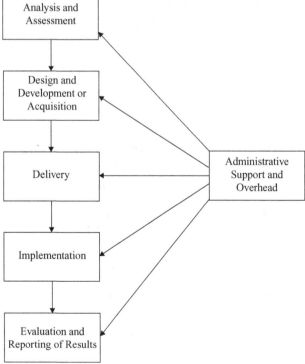

beginning with initial analysis and assessment and progressing to evaluation and reporting the results. These functional process steps represent the typical flow of work. After a performance problem is identified, a solution is developed or acquired and implemented within the organization. Implementation is often grouped with delivery. The entire process is routinely reported to the client or sponsor, and evaluation is undertaken to assess the program's success. There are also costs involved in supporting the entire process—administrative support and overhead costs. To fully understand the costs, the program should be analyzed according to these process categories, as described later in this chapter.

Prorated Versus Direct Costs

Usually, all costs related to a program are captured and expensed to that program. However, three categories are often prorated over several sessions of the same program. Needs assessment, design and development, and acquisition are all significant costs that should be prorated over the shelf life of a program. If the evaluators are using a conservative approach, the shelf life should be very short. Some organizations will prorate program costs over one year of operation; others may prorate costs over two or three years. If a dispute about the time period arises, the shorter period should be used. If possible, the finance and accounting staff should be consulted.

A brief example will illustrate how development costs are prorated. In a large pharmaceutical company, a program was developed at a cost of $150,000. It was anticipated that the program would have a three-year life before it would need to be updated. About nine hundred participants would be involved in the program over the three-year period, and an ROI calculation for fifty participants was planned. To be conservative, the total cost should be written off at the end of three years. Therefore, the $150,000 development cost would be spread over the nine hundred participants as a prorated development cost of $167 per participant. Thus, the ROI calculation for fifty participants would include a development cost of $8,350.

Employee Benefits Factor

When the cost of participant and staff time associated with programs is presented, the cost of employee benefits should be included along with the salary costs. Most organizations use a "benefits factor" to calculate the cost of benefits. The benefits factor is the cost of all employee benefits expressed as a percentage of total base salaries. This number is usually well known within an organization and typically has been generated by the human resources or finance and accounting staff for use in other costing applications. In some organizations, the benefits factor is as high as 50 percent or 60 percent. In others, it may be as low as 25 percent or 30 percent. The average in the United States is approximately 44 percent (U.S. Chamber of Commerce, 2006).

Major Cost Categories

The most important task in a tabulation of program costs is to define which costs should be included. These decisions will be made by the staff and usually approved by management. The finance and accounting staff may also need to approve the list. Table 2.3 shows the recommended cost categories for a fully loaded, conservative approach to estimating costs. Each category is described in this section.

Needs Assessment and Analysis

One cost category that is often overlooked is costs associated with conducting a needs assessment. In some programs, this cost is zero because the program is conducted without a needs assessment. However, as more organizations focus increased attention on needs assessments, this item will become a more significant cost. All costs associated with the needs assessment should be captured or estimated. These costs include the time of staff members who conduct the assessment, direct fees and expenses of external consultants who conduct the assessment, and internal services and supplies

Table 2.3. Recommended Cost Categories for Tabulation of Fully Loaded Program Costs

Cost Item	Prorated	Expensed
Needs assessment and analysis	√	
Design and development	√	
Acquisition	√	
Technological support	√	
Delivery and implementation		
Salaries and benefits, facilitators		√
Salaries and benefits, coordinators		√
Salaries and benefits, participants		√
Travel, lodging, meals		√
Facilities		√
Program materials and fees		√
Evaluation		√
Overhead	√	

used in the analysis. The total cost of the needs assessment is usually prorated over the life of the program. The estimated shelf life of the program should be kept reasonable—usually one to two years, depending on the nature of the program. The exception would be expensive programs and projects that are not expected to change significantly for several years.

Design and Development

One of the most significant cost categories is the costs associated with designing and developing a program. These costs include internal staff time for both design and development, as well as the cost of supplies, videos, software, and other material directly related to the program. These costs might also include consultant fees. Like needs assessment costs, design and development costs are usually prorated, perhaps using the same time frame. One to two years is recommended as the estimated shelf life of a program, unless the program is not expected to change for many years and the costs are significant.

When pilot programs are implemented, a prorating dilemma may surface. For expensive pilots, the complete design and development costs may be very significant. In this situation, prorating may not be an issue because the program is completely at risk. If all the costs are included in the ROI analysis, it may be difficult or impossible for a program to produce a positive ROI. The following rules can help evaluators work through this dilemma.

1. If the program is completely at risk, all the costs should be placed in the ROI evaluation decision. (That is, if the pilot does not have a positive ROI with all the costs included, the program will not be implemented.) This is rarely the case. However, if it is, the design and development costs should be kept to a minimum. Perhaps the program can be implemented without all the "bells and whistles." Development of videos, software, and other expensive tools can be delayed until the usefulness of the skills and content taught in the program is proven. Often, however, this approach is not feasible. Sometimes a program is developed in its entirety, but launched to an initial group in order to make adjustments before it is offered to the larger group. Rather than a true pilot, this is referred to as a "soft" launch, meaning that the program is not at risk.

2. If program implementation is not at risk, the cost of the development should be prorated over the anticipated life cycle of the program. This is the approach taken in most situations. Executives often find it reasonable to make a significant investment in the design and development of a pilot, with the understanding that if the program does not add value, it can be adjusted, changed, or modified so that it does add value. In these cases, a prorated development cost would be appropriate.

Regardless of the approach taken, it should be discussed during the planning stages, before the ROI evaluation begins. A dispute over prorating should not occur when the results are being tabulated. This discussion should also involve the sponsor of the program and a representative from finance and accounting.

Acquisition

In lieu of incurring development costs, some project leaders purchase programs to use directly or in a modified format. The acquisition costs for such programs include the purchase price for facilitator materials, train-the-trainer sessions, licensing agreements, and other costs associated with the right to deliver the program. These acquisition costs should be prorated using the same rationale that was detailed in earlier sections; an estimated shelf life of one to two years should be sufficient for acquired programs. If a program needs to be modified or some additional development is required, the associated costs should be categorized as development costs. In practice, many programs have both acquisition costs and development costs.

Technological Support

Some programs require technological support. For example, computers may be used to deliver the content of a program. The finance and accounting department can provide information on how to spread the costs of technology over the life of a program based on how the equipment is depreciated. Some programs are associated with new work processes or implementation of technology that require the use of a help desk for a period of time following the program. When it is appropriate to capture these costs, they may also be prorated over the life of the program.

Delivery and Implementation

Usually the largest segment of program costs are those associated with delivery or implementation. Five major subcategories are discussed in this section.

Facilitators' and Coordinators' Salaries and Benefits

The salaries of facilitators or program coordinators should be included in the program's cost. Salaries should be proportionally allocated according to how much time was spent on a program. If a coordinator is involved in more than one program, that person's time should be proportionally allocated to the specific program under review. If external facilitators are used, all charges for the session should be included. The important issue is to capture all the direct time of internal employees or external consultants who work directly with the program. Each time direct labor costs are involved, the benefits factor should be used to figure the cost of employee benefits so that it can be included. As we discussed earlier in this chapter, the benefits factor is usually in the range of 30 to 50 percent in the United States.

Participants' Salaries and Benefits

The salaries and benefits of participants are an expense that should be included in the program cost. Again, they should be allocated according to how much time was spent participating in the program. For situations in which the program has already been conducted, these costs can be estimated by using average or midpoint values for the salaries in typical job classifications. When a program is targeted for an ROI calculation, participants can provide their salaries directly and confidentially.

Travel, Lodging, and Meals

Direct travel costs for participants, facilitators, and coordinators should be included in the program cost. Lodging and meals for participants, facilitators, and coordinators during travel, as well as meals during their stay for the program, should also be included. Refreshments should be included in the program cost as well.

Facilities

The cost of the facilities should be included in the program cost. For meetings or sessions held at external facilities, this cost is the direct charge from the conference center or hotel. If the program is conducted in-house, the use of the conference room represents a cost for the organization, and that cost should be estimated and included even if it is not the practice within the organization to include in-house facilities' costs in other reports. The cost of internal facilities can easily be estimated by obtaining the rental rate of a room of the same size at a local hotel. Sometimes, a cost figure, calculated on a square footage basis, is available from the finance and accounting staff or the facilities management team (that is, the cost of organizational facilities per square foot per day). In other situations, the cost of commercial real estate on a square footage basis can be determined from commercial real estate agents or the local newspaper. The important point is to come quickly to a credible estimate for the cost of the room.

The cost of facilities is an important issue that is often overlooked. With encouragement from the finance and accounting staff, some staff members do not show an amount for the use of internal facilities, arguing that the overhead cost of the room would be regardless. However, the complete cost of a program should include this item, because the room would probably be used for other purposes if programs were not conducted. In the total cost picture, this is a very minor charge. The fact of its being included might be of more value from a credibility standpoint than from the standpoint of its influence on the ROI calculation.

Program Materials and Fees

Specific program materials such as notebooks, textbooks, how-to manuals, instruction guides, software, case studies, exercises, and participant workbooks should be included in the delivery costs of a program, along with license fees, user fees, and royalty payments. Pens, paper, certificates, calculators, and personal copies of software are also included in this category.

For major programs, implementation may be a separate cost category. If the program involves meetings, follow-ups, manager reinforcement, or other activities beyond the program, an additional category for implementation may be appropriate. In some cases, on-site coordinators are available to provide assistance and support for employees as the program is implemented throughout the region, branch, or division. The total cost of these coordinators is an implementation expense that should be included in the program cost.

The specific cost categories for implementation often mirror the categories for delivery. However, in most situations, the implementation is considered part of the delivery and is placed in that category. The remainder of this book presents delivery and implementation as a combined category.

Evaluation

Usually, the total evaluation cost is included in the program cost so that the figure is fully loaded. Evaluation costs include the cost of developing the evaluation strategy, designing instruments, collecting data, data analysis, and report preparation and distribution. Cost categories include time, materials, hardware or software used to collect or analyze data, and purchased instruments or surveys. A case can be made for prorating evaluation costs over several programs instead of charging the total amount as an expense to one program. For example, twenty-five sessions of a program are conducted in a three-year period, and one group is selected for an ROI calculation. The costs of the ROI evaluation could logically be prorated over the twenty-five sessions because the results of the ROI analysis should reflect the success of the other programs and will perhaps result in changes that will affect the other programs as well.

Overhead

A final charge is the cost of overhead, the additional costs within the functional unit that are not directly related to a particular program. The overhead category represents any department costs not considered in the preceding categories. Typical overhead items include the cost of clerical support, departmental office expenses, salaries of managers, and other fixed costs. Some organizations obtain an estimate for overhead allocation by dividing the total overhead by an appropriate number in order to prorate the costs. The number may be the total participants or programs during the year. The result becomes a standard value to use in calculations.

An example will illustrate the simplicity of prorating overhead costs. An organization with fifty training and development programs tabulated all the expenditures in the budget not allocated directly to a particular program ($548,061). This part of the budget represented total overhead. Next, this number was divided by the total number of participant days or hours (for example, if a five-day program is offered ten times a year, 50 days would be put in the total days category, or 400 hours in the total hours category, based on an eight-hour workday). Using participant hours may be helpful if there is a significant amount of e-learning and participants are involved in programs an hour at a time. In other situations, allocation of participant days may be appropriate. In this example, participant days for the year totaled approximately 7,400. The total unallocated overhead of $548,061 was divided by 7,400 days to arrive at $74. Therefore, $74 is charged for overhead for each day of training. A three-day leadership program would be charged $222 for overhead. The overhead amount is usually small and will have very little impact on the ROI calculation. However, including overhead cost as part of a fully loaded cost profile builds credibility with sponsors and senior executives.

Another example illustrates a slightly different approach. In this case, the overhead for a human resources unit is needed in order to place a value on an individual's participation in a human resources (HR) program. Exhibit 2.1 summarizes the relevant information. For simplicity, a $1 million HR budget is assumed and it is estimated that $200,000 of that budget is not allocated to specific programs. The total number of participants in all HR programs (with some duplication) is 8,000. Therefore, the allocation per participant is $25. Thus, if a program is destined for an ROI calculation and 500

Exhibit 2.1. Example of Overhead Allocation

Total HR budget:	$1,000,000
Portion of budget not allocated to specific HR programs:	$200,000
Total number of participants in HR programs:	8,000
Allocation per participant:	$25

people participate, then the amount of overhead allocated to the program would be 500 × $25, or $12,500.

The key to allocating overhead is to use a simple approach that logically and systematically allocates the costs in the department that are not allocated to specific programs. Also, it is important not to spend too much time on this issue. Estimates are appropriate in most situations. Some organizations estimate an amount of overhead for a program, using some logical rationale, spending no more than ten or fifteen minutes on the issue. The overhead will not be a deal breaker in the ROI calculation for most programs.

Cost Reporting

An example from an actual case shows how total program costs are presented. Table 2.4 shows the cost of a major executive leadership program. The extensive program involved four one-week, off-site training sessions in which personal coaches and learning coaches were assigned to the participants. Working in teams, participants tackled a project that was important to top executives. Each team reported their results to management. The project teams could hire consultants as well. These costs are listed as program costs. The costs for the first group of twenty-two participants are detailed in the table.

The issue of prorating costs was an important consideration. In this case, it was reasonably certain that a second group would participate in the program; therefore, the analysis, design, and development expenses of $580,657 could be prorated over two sessions. As

Table 2.4. Reporting of Fully Loaded Costs for an Executive Leadership Development Program

Analysis, Design, and Development	
External consultants	$ 525,330
Training department salaries and benefits	
(for direct work on the program)	28,785
Management committee salaries and benefits	
(for direct work on the program)	26,542
Delivery	
Conference facilities (hotel)	142,554
External consultants	812,110
Training department salaries and benefits	
(for direct work on the program)	15,283
Training department travel expenses	37,500
Management committee	
(for direct work on the program)	75,470
Program costs ($25,000 × 4 weeks)	100,000
Participant salaries and benefits (class sessions)	
(average daily salary × benefits factor × number	
of program days)	84,564
Participant salaries and benefits (program work)	117,353
Travel and lodging for participants	100,938
Cost of materials (handouts, purchased materials)	6,872
Research and Evaluation	
Research	110,750
Evaluation	125,875
Total costs	$2,309,926

a result, in the actual ROI calculation, half of the total cost figure ($290,328) was used as the cost for analysis, design, and development. This left a total program cost of $2,019,598 ($2,309,926 − $290,328) to include in the analysis. This total represented $91,800 per participant, or $22,950 per participant for each week of formal sessions. Although this program was very expensive, it was close to a rough benchmark for weekly costs of other senior executive leadership programs.

Cost Accumulation and Estimation

There are two basic ways to accumulate costs. One is to categorize them according to the nature of the expenditure—for example, labor, materials, supplies, travel, and so on. These are expense account classifications. The other is to categorize costs according to the process or function that they apply to—for example, program development, delivery, or evaluation. An effective system monitors costs in expense account categories but also includes a method for accumulating costs in process or functional categories. However, in practice, many systems stop short of this second step. While the first grouping is sufficient to provide a total program cost, it does not allow useful comparison with other programs in order to identify areas in which costs might be excessive.

Cost Classification Matrix

Costs are accumulated in both expense account and functional classifications. The two are obviously related, and the relationship depends on the organization. For instance, the specific costs involved in analysis of a program may vary substantially from organization to organization.

An important part of the classification process is to define the kinds of costs in the account classification system that normally fall in each of the process or functional categories. Table 2.5 is a matrix that shows the categories for accumulating all program-related costs within a particular organization. The costs that normally fall in each process or functional category are checked in the matrix.

Each member of a program team should know how to charge expenses properly. For example, if equipment is rented to use in the development and delivery of a program, should all or part of the cost be charged to development? Or should it be charged to

Table 2.5. Cost Classification Matrix for Program-Related Costs

	Process or Functional Categories				
Expense Account Classification	Analysis	Development	Delivery	Operations and Maintenance	Evaluation
00 Salaries and benefits—department staff	X	X	X	X	X
01 Salaries and benefits—other staff		X	X		
02 Salaries and benefits—participants			X	X	X
03 Meals, travel, and incidental expenses—department staff	X	X	X	X	X
04 Meals, travel, and accommodations—participants			X		
05 Office supplies and expenses	X	X	X	X	X
06 Program materials and supplies		X			
07 Printing and reproduction	X	X	X	X	X
08 Outside services	X	X	X	X	X
09 Equipment expenses	X	X	X	X	X
10 Equipment—rental			X	X	
11 Equipment—maintenance		X	X	X	
12 Registration fees	X				
13 Facilities expense allocation			X	X	
14 Facilities rental			X		
15 General overhead allowance	X	X	X	X	X
16 Other miscellaneous expenses	X	X	X	X	X

delivery? More than likely, the cost will be allocated in proportion to the extent to which the item was used for each function.

Cost Accumulation

With expense account classifications clearly defined and the process or functional categories determined, tracking the costs of individual programs is easy. This feat is accomplished by using account numbers and program numbers. The following example illustrates the use of these numbers.

A program number is a three-digit number representing a specific program. Here are some examples:

New professional on-boarding	112
New team leader training	215
Statistical quality control	418
Valuing diversity	791

Numbers are assigned to the process or functional categories. Using the example presented earlier, the following numbers are assigned.

Analysis	1
Development	2
Delivery	3
Operations and maintenance	4
Evaluation	5

The two-digit numbers assigned to account classifications in the left-hand column in Table 2.5 complete the accounting system. For example, if workbooks are reproduced for a statistical quality control workshop, the appropriate charge number for that reproduction is 07-3-418. The first two digits denote the account classification (printing and reproduction); the next digit indicates the process or functional category (delivery); and the last three digits are the program number (statistical quality control). This system enables rapid accumulation and monitoring of program costs. Total costs can then be presented by

- Program (for example, statistical quality control)

- Process or functional category (for example, delivery)

- Expense account classification (for example, printing and reproduction)

Cost Estimation

The preceding sections cover procedures for classifying and monitoring costs related to programs. Monitoring and comparing ongoing costs with the budget or with projected costs is important. However, a significant reason for tracking costs is to predict the cost of future programs. Usually, this goal is accomplished through a formal cost estimation method that is unique to an organization.

Some organizations use cost estimating worksheets to arrive at the total cost for a proposed program. Exhibit 2.2 shows a cost estimating worksheet that summarizes analysis, development, delivery, operations and maintenance, and evaluation costs. The worksheet contains a few formulas that make it easier to estimate the costs. In addition to cost estimating worksheets, organizations often provide the current rates for services, supplies, and salaries. These data become outdated quickly and are usually updated periodically.

The most appropriate way to predict costs is by tracking the actual costs incurred in all phases—from analysis to evaluation—of all programs. This way, it is possible to see how much is spent on programs and how much is being spent in the different categories. Until adequate cost data are available, however, detailed analysis on the worksheets for cost estimation will be necessary.

Exhibit 2.2. Cost Estimating Worksheet

Cost Items	Total
Analysis Costs	
Salaries and employee benefits—department staff (number of people × average hourly salary × employee benefits factor × number of hours on project)	____
Meals, travel, and incidental expenses	____
Office supplies and expenses	____
Printing and reproduction	____
Outside services	____
Equipment expenses	____
Registration fees	____
Other miscellaneous expenses	____
Total Analysis Cost	____
Development Costs	
Salaries and employee benefits—department staff (number of people × average hourly salary × employee benefits factor × number of hours on project)	____
Salaries and employee benefits—other staff	____
Meals, travel, and incidental expenses	____
Office supplies and expenses	____
Program materials and supplies	____
Printing and reproduction	____
Outside services	____
Equipment expenses	____
Other miscellaneous expenses	____
Total Development Cost	____
Delivery Costs	
Salaries and employee benefits—participants (number of participants × average hourly or daily salary × employee benefits factor × hours or days on project)	____
Meals, travel, and accommodations—participants (number of participants × average daily expenses × number of days on project)	____

Exhibit 2.2. Cost Estimating Worksheet (*Continued*)

Cost Items	Total
Program materials and supplies	___
Printing and reproduction	___
Participant replacement costs (if applicable)	___
Lost production (explain basis)	___
Facilitator costs	
Salaries and benefits	___
Meals, travel, and incidental expenses	___
Outside services	___
Facility costs	
Facilities rental	___
Facilities expense allocation	___
Equipment expenses	___
Other miscellaneous expenses	___
Total Delivery Cost	___

Operations and Maintenance

Salaries and employee benefits—department staff (number of people × average hourly or daily salary × employee benefits factor × number of hours on project)	___
Meals, travel, and incidental expenses	___
Salaries and employee benefits—participants (number of participants × average hourly or daily salary × employee benefits factor × hours or days spent on project)	___
Office supplies and expenses	___
Outside services	___
Equipment expenses	___
Other miscellaneous expenses	___
Total Operations and Maintenance Cost	___

Evaluation Costs

Salaries and employee benefits—department staff (number of people × average hourly or daily salary × employee benefits factor × number of hours on project)	___
Meals, travel, and incidental expenses	___

(*Continued*)

Exhibit 2.2. Cost Estimating Worksheet (*Continued*)

Cost Items	Total
Salaries and employee benefits—participants (number of participants × average hourly or daily salary × employee benefits factor × hours or days on project)	____
Office supplies and expenses	____
Printing and reproduction	____
Outside services	____
Equipment expenses	____
Other miscellaneous expenses	____
Total Evaluation Cost	____
General Overhead Allocation	____
Total Program Cost	____

Case Study: Federal Information Agency

To illustrate the importance of tracking costs and detailing them, the following case study is presented in its entirety. The introductory and explanatory material is presented so that the complete costs can be better appreciated. As a practice exercise, the costs, representing three years of data, should be entered on the cost worksheet shown in Exhibit 2.3. The completed cost worksheet is shown at the end of the case study.

Overview

The Federal Information Agency (FIA) provides information to other government agencies and businesses as well as state and local organizations, agencies, and interested groups. Several hundred communication specialists with backgrounds in information systems, computer science, electrical engineering, and information science operate across the United States in order to perform their work. Almost all the specialists have bachelor's degrees in one of

Exhibit 2.3. Cost Worksheet

	Year 1	Year 2	Year 3	Total
Initial analysis (prorated)	——	——	——	——
Development (prorated)	——	——	——	——
Tuition—regular	——	——	——	——
Tuition—premium	——	——	——	——
Salaries and benefits—participants	——	——	——	——
Salaries and benefits—program administrator	——	——	——	——
Program coordination	——	——	——	——
Facilities	——	——	——	——
Salaries and benefits—managers	——	——	——	——
Evaluation	——	——	——	——
Total	——	——	——	——

these fields. The headquarters and operation center where 1,500 of the specialists are employed is in the Washington, D.C., area.

Problem and Solution

FIA was experiencing two problems that had senior agency officials concerned. The first problem was an unacceptable rate of employee turnover among the communication specialists—the rate averaged 38 percent in the year before the program was implemented. The need to recruit and train replacements due to the high rate of turnover was placing a strain on the agency. An analysis of exit interviews indicated that employees left primarily for higher salaries. Because FIA was somewhat constrained in its ability to increase salaries, competing with the salaries and benefits offered in the private sector had become difficult. Although salary increases and adjustments in pay levels would be necessary in order to lower turnover, FIA was also exploring other options.

The second problem concerned the need to continually update the technical skills of the staff. While the vast majority of the 1,500 specialists had a bachelor's degree, only a few had a master's degree in their specialty. In this work environment, formal education was quickly outdated. The annual feedback survey of employees indicated a strong interest in an in-house master's degree program in information science. Therefore, FIA explored the possibility of offering such a program. The program would be conducted by the School of Engineering and Science at Regional State University (RSU), and it would be implemented at no cost to the participating employees and conducted on the agency's time during regular work hours. Designed to address both employee turnover and skill updates, the program would normally take three years for participants to complete.

Program Description

RSU was selected to offer the master's program because of its reputation and because its curriculum matched FIA's needs. The program allowed participants to take one or two courses per semester. Taking two courses per semester schedule would enable participants to complete the program in three years. Both morning and afternoon classes were available, each representing three hours per week of class time. Participants were discouraged from taking more than two courses per term. Although a thesis option was normally available at RSU, FIA requested that a graduate project for six hours of credit be required instead of a thesis. The project would begin in Year 2 of the program. A professor would supervise the project. Designed to add value, the project would be applied within the agency.

Classes were usually taught live by professors at the agency's center. Participants were asked to prepare for classroom activities on their own time but were allowed to attend classes on the agency's time. A typical three-year schedule for the program is shown in Table 2.6.

Senior management approved the master's degree curriculum, which represented a mix of courses normally offered in the program

Table 2.6. Typical Three-Year Schedule for Master's Program in Information Science at the Federal Information Agency

	Year 1	Year 2	Year 3
Fall	2 courses (6 hours)	2 courses (6 hours)	2 courses (6 hours)
Spring	2 courses (6 hours)	2 courses (6 hours)	2 courses (6 hours)
Summer	1 course (3 hours)	1 course (3 hours) Graduate project (3 hours)	Graduate project (3 hours)

Total semester hours: 48

and others specially selected for FIA staff. Two new courses were designed by university faculty for the curriculum. These two represented a slight modification of existing courses and were tailored to the communication requirements of the agency. Elective courses were not allowed, for two reasons. First, it would complicate the offerings, requiring additional courses, facilities, and professors—and adding costs to the program. Second, FIA wanted a prescribed, customized curriculum that would add value to the agency while meeting the requirements of the university.

Selection Criteria

An important issue involved the selection of employees to participate in the program. Most employees who voluntarily left the agency resigned within the first four years and were often considered to have high potential for advancement within the agency. Taking these considerations into account, the program designers established the following criteria in order to identify and select employees for the program.

1. A candidate must have at least one year of service prior to beginning classes.

2. A candidate must meet the normal requirements for acceptance into the graduate school at the university.

3. A candidate must be willing to sign a commitment to stay with the agency for two years beyond program completion.

4. A candidate's immediate manager must nominate the employee for consideration.

5. A candidate must be rated "high potential" by the immediate manager.

The management team was provided initial information on the program, kept informed of its development and progress prior to its launch, and briefed as selection criteria were finalized. It was emphasized that selection of participants should be based on objective criteria, following the guidelines offered. At the same time, managers were asked to provide feedback on the level of interest and specific issues about the nomination of candidates.

One hundred participants per year were allowed to enter the program. This limit was based on two key issues:

1. The ability of the university to staff the program had limits; RSU could not effectively teach more than one hundred participants each semester.

2. The program was an experiment that could be modified or enhanced in the future if it was successful.

Program Administration

Because of the magnitude of the anticipated enrollment, FIA appointed a full-time program administrator who was responsible for organizing and coordinating the program. The administrator's duties included registration of the participants, all correspondence and communication with the university and participants, facilities and logistics (including materials and books), and resolving problems as they occurred. FIA absorbed the total cost of the coordinator. The university assigned an individual to serve as a liaison with the agency. This individual was not an additional hire, and the university absorbed the cost of the liaison's time as part of the cost of doing business, covered by tuition.

Drivers of Evaluation

The in-house master's program was selected for comprehensive evaluation. The program's impact on the agency would be assessed, using a four-year time frame. Several influences had brought about the mandate for such detailed accountability.

1. Senior administrators had requested detailed evaluations for certain programs that were considered strategic and that were highly visible and designed to add a great deal of value to the agency.
2. This program was perceived to be very expensive; thus, senior management demanded a higher level of accountability, including return on investment.
3. Because retention was a critical issue for the agency, it was important to determine whether this solution was the appropriate one. A detailed measurement and evaluation would assess the success of the program.
4. The passage of federal legislation and other initiatives aimed at providing more accountability for the use of taxpayers' funds had resulted in a shift toward more public sector accountability in the United States.

As a result, the implementation team planned a detailed evaluation of the master's program that went beyond traditional program evaluation processes. In addition to tracking costs, the team would determine the monetary payoff, including the ROI. Because the master's program was a very complex and comprehensive solution, other important measures would be tracked in order to provide a balanced approach to the measurement.

Recognizing the shift toward public sector accountability, the human resources staff had developed the necessary skills to implement the ROI Methodology; a small group of HR staff members had been certified to implement the ROI Methodology within the agency.

Program Costs

The costs of the program were tabulated and monitored. The evaluation used a fully loaded cost profile, which included all direct and indirect costs. One of the major costs was the tuition for the participants. The university charged the customary tuition, which included the cost of books and materials plus $100 per semester course per participant to offset the additional travel expenses and the faculty expenses of conducting and coordinating the program. The tuition per semester hour was $200 (that is, $600 per three-hour course).

The full-time program administrator was an FIA employee, receiving a base salary of $37,000 per year, with a 45 percent employee benefits factor. The administrator had expenses of approximately $15,000 per year.

Salaries for the participants represented another significant cost category. The average salary for the job categories of the employees involved in the program was $47,800, with a 45 percent employee benefits factor. Salaries usually increased approximately 4 percent per year. Participants attended class a total of 18 hours for each semester hour of credit. Therefore, a three-hour course represented 54 hours of off-the-job time in the classroom. The total hours of off-the-job class time needed for one participant to complete the program was 756 hours (14 courses × 54 hours).

Classroom facilities were another significant cost category. For the one hundred participants, four different courses were offered each semester, and each course was repeated at a different time.

With a class size of twenty-five, eight separate semester courses were presented. Although the classrooms used for this program were normally used for other training and education programs offered at the agency, the cost of providing the facilities was included. (Because of the unusual demand, an additional conference room was built in order to provide ample meeting space.) The estimate for the average cost of all meeting rooms was $40 per hour of use.

The cost of the initial assessment that led to the program, including the turnover analysis, was included in the cost profile. This charge, estimated to be $5,000, was prorated for the first three years. FIA's development costs for the program were estimated to be $10,000 and were also prorated for three years. Management time spent on the program was minimal but was estimated to cost $9,000 over the three-year period. Management time was primarily spent on attending meetings and writing memos about the program. Finally, the evaluation costs, representing the cost of tracking the success of the program and reporting the results to management, were estimated to be $10,000 (see Exhibit 2.4).

Final Thoughts

Costs are important in a variety of applications. Tracking costs helps program staff manage resources carefully, consistently, and efficiently. Tracking costs also allows comparisons between cost items and cost categories over time or across projects. There are several systems of cost categorization; the most common ones are presented in this chapter.

Costs should be fully loaded for an ROI calculation. From a practical standpoint, including certain cost items may be optional because of an organization's cost guidelines or cost philosophy. However, because ROI calculations are often closely scrutinized,

Exhibit 2.4. Completed Cost Worksheet for FIA's In-House Master's Program

	Year 1	Year 2	Year 3	Total
Initial analysis (prorated)	$1,667	$1,667	$1,666	$5,000
Development (prorated)	3,333	3,333	3,334	10,000
Tuition—regular	300,000	342,000	273,000	915,000
Tuition—premium	50,000	57,000	45,500	152,500
Salaries and benefits—participants	899,697	888,900	708,426	2,497,023
Salaries and benefits—program administrator	53,650	55,796	58,028	167,474
Program coordination	15,000	15,000	15,000	45,000
Facilities	43,200	43,200	34,560	120,960
Salaries and benefits—managers	3,000	3,000	3,000	9,000
Evaluation	3,333	3,333	3,334	10,000
Total	$1,372,880	$1,413,229	$1,145,848	$3,931,957

all costs should be included, even if their inclusion goes beyond the requirements of an organization's policy.

References

ROI Institute. *ROI Certification Handbook.* Birmingham, Ala.: ROI Institute, 2005.

U.S. Chamber of Commerce. *Annual Employee Benefits Study.* Washington, D.C.: U.S. Chamber of Commerce, 2006.

3

The ROI Calculation

The monetary values for the program benefits (described in *Data Conversion*, book four of this series) are combined with program cost data (described in Chapter Two of this book) to calculate return on investment (ROI). This chapter explores several approaches to calculating ROI, describing the techniques, processes, and issues involved. Before presenting the formulas for calculating ROI and benefit-cost ratio (BCR), this chapter discusses a few basic issues. An adequate understanding of these issues is necessary to complete an ROI calculation, one of the major steps in the ROI Methodology. The uses and abuses of ROI are also fully explored in this chapter.

Basic Issues in Calculating ROI

Before presenting the methods for calculating ROI, we will review a few issues that are key to understanding the calculation process and the ROI values.

Definitions Are Critical

The term *return on investment* is often misused, sometimes intentionally. In some situations, ROI is defined broadly to mean any benefit from a program. In these situations, ROI is a vague concept in which even the most elusive data associated with a program are included in the concept of return on investment. In this book, *return on investment* is a precise term, signifying an actual value that is calculated by comparing a program's costs with its benefits. The two most common measures of return on investment are the benefit-cost ratio and the ROI formula. Both are presented in this chapter.

For many years, practitioners and researchers have sought to calculate the actual return on investment for all types of programs and projects. For example, if formal employee learning and development is considered an investment, not an expense, then learning and development investments should be subject to the same funding mechanism as other investments, such as the investments in equipment and facilities. Although investments in learning are quite different from these other investments, management often views them in the same way. Therefore, developing specific measures that reflect the return on the investment in learning and development programs is critical to the success of the field of learning and development.

Annualized Values

All the formulas presented in this chapter use annualized values, which means that the impact of the program investment in the first year is measured. Using annual values is becoming a generally accepted practice in evaluating ROI in many organizations. This practice is a conservative approach to measuring ROI, because many short-term programs continue to add value in the second or third year after they are implemented. For long-term programs, annualized values are inappropriate and longer time frames need to be used. For example, in an ROI analysis of a program to send employees to the United States to obtain MBA degrees, a Singapore-based company used a seven-year time frame. The program itself required two years, after which post-program impact data were collected over five years and eventually used to calculate the ROI for the program. However, for most programs lasting one day to one month, basing values on the program's impact in the first year is appropriate.

When selecting the approach to measuring ROI, it is important to communicate to the target audience the formula used and the assumptions made in deciding to use it. This action can avoid misunderstandings and confusion about how the ROI value was developed. Although several approaches are described in this chapter, two stand out as preferred methods: the benefit-cost ratio and the basic ROI formula. These two approaches are described next, along with the interpretation of ROI and brief coverage of other approaches.

Benefit-Cost Ratio

One of the earliest methods for evaluating investments is the benefit-cost ratio. This method compares the benefits of a program to its costs. The ratio is expressed in this formula:

$$BCR = \frac{\text{Program Benefits}}{\text{Program Costs}}$$

In simple terms, the BCR compares the annual economic benefits of a program to the costs of the program. A BCR of 1, written 1:1, means that the benefits equal the costs. A BCR of 2, written 2:1, indicates that for each dollar spent on the program, two dollars in benefits were returned.

The following example illustrates the use of the benefit-cost ratio. A large metropolitan bus system introduced a new program to reduce unscheduled absences. An increase in absences had left the system facing many delays; to prevent the delays, a large pool of drivers had been created to fill in for the absent drivers. The pool had become substantial, representing a significant expenditure. The program involved a change in policy and a change in the selection process for regular drivers, coupled with meetings and communication. Significant improvements were generated. The benefits of the program were captured in a one-year follow-up and compared with the total cost of the program. The benefits from the first year of the program were valued at $662,000. The fully loaded implementation costs totaled $67,400. Thus, the benefit-cost ratio is as follows:

$$BCR = \frac{\$662,000}{\$67,400} = 9.82$$

For every dollar invested in this program, almost ten dollars in benefits were returned. Later in this chapter, the ROI for this program will be calculated.

The BCR is not a traditional financial measure, so no confusion arises when comparing program investments with investments in plants, equipment, or subsidiaries, which use other indicators in the cost-benefit comparison. Some managers prefer not to use the same method to evaluate the return on their program investments that is used to evaluate the return on other investments.

There are no standards for what constitutes an acceptable benefit-cost ratio. A standard should be established within an organization; however, in some organizations, the standard may vary depending on the type of program. Nonetheless, a 1:1 benefit-cost ratio, reflecting break-even return, is unacceptable for most programs, and in some organizations, a 1.25:1 benefit-cost ratio is required, signifying that 1.25 times the cost of the program is the required benefit.

ROI Formula

Another common formula for evaluating program investments is net program benefits divided by costs. The ratio is expressed as a percentage, so the value yielded by the basic formula is multiplied by 100. The formula for ROI is as follows:

$$ROI(\%) = \frac{\text{Net Program Benefits}}{\text{Program Costs}} \times 100$$

Net benefits are the program benefits minus program costs. The ROI value can be obtained from the BCR by subtracting one. For example, a BCR of 2.45 is the same as an ROI value of 1.45, or 145 percent.

This ROI formula is essentially the same as the ROI formula for other types of investments. For example, when a firm builds a new plant, the ROI is calculated by dividing annual earnings by the investment. The annual earnings (annual revenue minus expenses) are comparable to net benefits (annual benefits minus costs). The investment is comparable to program costs, which are the investment in the program.

An ROI of 50 percent for a program means that the costs have been recovered and an additional amount equal to 50 percent of the costs has been gained as "earnings." So, if one dollar is invested, the dollar would be recovered plus an additional fifty cents. An ROI of 150 percent indicates that the costs have been recovered and additional "earnings" equal to 1.5 times the costs have been received. In other words, for every dollar invested, the dollar investment is recovered plus a gain of an additional one dollar and fifty cents.

The following example illustrates the ROI calculation. Hewlett-Packard took a unique approach to increasing telephone-based sales (Seagraves, 2001). An innovative, multistep sales skills intervention drove tremendous improvement in sales skills. The sales improvement, when translated into increased profit, yielded impressive results. The monetary benefits were $3,296,977, and the total, fully loaded costs were $1,116,291. Thus, the net benefits were $2,180,686 ($3,296,977 − $1,116,291). The ROI calculation looks like this:

$$\text{ROI(\%)} = \frac{\$2,180,686}{\$1,116,291} \times 100 = 195\%$$

After the costs of the program had been recovered, Hewlett-Packard received almost two dollars for each dollar invested.

Using the ROI formula places program investments on a level playing field with other investments by using the same formula and similar concepts. The ROI calculation is easily understood by key management and financial executives, who regularly use the ROI formula to evaluate other investments.

ROI Examples

To illustrate how the ROI and BCR calculations are developed, five brief examples are presented in this section. Some of these cases are briefly discussed in some of the other books in this series. Here, the ROI calculations from the cases are presented, showing the monetary results of each program. Working through these examples to become familiar with what goes into the analysis and the actual calculations may be helpful.

Example 1: Retail Merchandise Company

Retail Merchandise Company (RMC), a large national store chain located in most major markets in the United States, piloted a program to boost sales by teaching interactive selling skills to sales associates. The program, developed and delivered by an outside vendor, was a response to a clearly identified need to increase interaction between sales associates and customers. The program consisted of two days of skills training, followed by three weeks of on-the-job skill application. The third day of the program was used for follow-up and additional training. Three groups representing the electronics departments of three stores were initially trained in a pilot implementation. A total of forty-eight employees participated.

Post-program data collection was accomplished through three methods. First, the average weekly sales of each associate were monitored (business performance monitoring of output data). Second, a follow-up questionnaire was distributed three months after the program was completed in order to assess Level 3 success (actual application of skills on the job). Third, Level 3 data were solicited in a follow-up session, which was conducted on the third day of the program. In this session, participants disclosed their success (or lack of success) in applying the new skills. They also discussed the techniques they used to overcome the barriers to program implementation.

The method used to isolate the effects of the program was a control group arrangement. Three store locations (control group) were identified and compared with the three groups that participated in the pilot program (experimental group). The variables of previous store performance, annual sales volume, average household disposable income in the area, and customer traffic levels were used to match the two groups so that they could be as similar as possible. The method of converting data to monetary values was extrapolation of direct profit contribution, based on the value of increased output. The amount of profit that resulted from one additional dollar of sales (profit margin) was a readily available figure that was used in the calculation.

Although the program was evaluated at all five levels outlined in the ROI Methodology, the emphasis of this study was on Levels 4 and 5. The data at Levels 1, 2, and 3 met or exceeded expectations. Table 3.1 shows the Level 4 data—the average weekly sales of both groups after the program. For convenience and at the request of management, a three-month follow-up period was used. Management wanted to implement the program at other locations if it appeared to be successful in the first three months of operation. Evaluation after three months may be premature in terms of determining the total impact of the program, but in practice, evaluation after three months is common because it is convenient. Data from the first three weeks after the program are shown in Table 3.1, along with data from the last three weeks of the evaluation period (weeks 13, 14, and 15). The data show what appears to be a significant difference in the two values.

Two steps were required to move from the Level 4 impact data to Level 5, ROI evaluation. First, the Level 4 data had to be converted to monetary values. Second, the costs of the program had to be tabulated.

First, we will discuss the conversion of the data to monetary values. Exhibit 3.1 shows the annualized program benefits. Only forty-six participants were still in their job after three months; to be

Table 3.1. Level 4 Data: Average Weekly Sales per Associate

Weeks After Program	Post-Program Data for Experimental Groups	Post-Program Data for Control Groups
1	$9,723	$9,698
2	9,978	9,720
3	10,424	9,812
13	13,690	11,572
14	11,491	9,683
15	11,044	10,092
Average for weeks 13, 14, 15	$12,075	$10,449

conservative, the other two participants' potential improvements were excluded from the benefits. The profit contribution at the store level, obtained from the accounting department, was 2 percent of sales. Out of every dollar of additional sales attributed to the program, only two cents would be considered added value.

First-year values were used to reflect the total impact of the program. The annual benefits were calculated using forty-eight weeks rather than fifty-two weeks to account for holidays and vacation. Ideally, if new skills had been acquired, as the Level 3 evaluation

Exhibit 3.1. Annualized Program Benefits

Number of participants who were still in their job after three months: 46

Average weekly sales per associate—program groups	$12,075
Average weekly sales per associate—control groups	10,449
Increase in weekly sales per associate	1,626
Profit contribution from sales increase (2% of sales)	32.50
Total weekly improvement in profit ($32.50 × 46 associates)	1,495
Total annual benefits ($1495 × 48 weeks)	$71,760

Table 3.2. Cost Summary

Item	Cost
Facilitation fees (3 courses @ $3,750)	$11,250
Program materials (48 sets @ $35)	1,680
Meals and refreshments (3 days @ $28/participant)	4,032
Facilities (9 days @ $120)	1,080
Participants' salaries plus benefits (35% of salaries)	12,442
Coordination and evaluation	2,500
Total costs	$32,984

Note: There were forty-eight participants in three courses.

indicated, some value from the use of those skills would occur in the second year or perhaps even in the third year after program implementation. However, for short-term programs, only first-year values are used, requiring the investment to have an acceptable return in a one-year time period. Thus, Guiding Principle 9 states, "Use only the first year of annual benefits in ROI analysis of short-term solutions." The total benefits were $71,760.

Second, we address the tabulation of costs. Table 3.2 shows the cost summary for this program. Costs were fully loaded, including data for all forty-eight participants. The need for the program was identified by senior managers, so a formal needs assessment was not conducted. Since an external supplier conducted the program, there were no direct development costs. The facilitation fee covered the prorated development costs as well as the delivery costs.

The participants' salaries plus a 35 percent factor for employee benefits were included in the costs. Facilities costs were included, although the company did not normally capture the costs when internal facilities were used, as they were for this program. The estimated cost for coordination and evaluation of the program was also included. The total cost of the program was $32,984. Thus, the benefit-cost ratio was as follows:

$$\text{BCR} = \frac{\$71,760}{\$32,984} = 2.18{:}1$$

And the ROI was as follows:

$$\text{ROI}(\%) = \frac{\$71,760 - \$32,984}{\$32,984} \times 100 = 118\%$$

The acceptable ROI, defined by the client, was 25 percent. Therefore, the pilot program had an excellent ROI after three months of on-the-job skill applications. As a result, the decision to implement the program throughout the other store locations became much easier. Six types of data had been collected to show the full range of success, including the actual ROI.

This example, in which the payoff on a pilot program was developed, represents an excellent use of the ROI Methodology. Historically, the decision to go from pilot to full implementation is often based on reaction (Level 1) data alone. Sometimes, learning (Level 2) data and, in limited cases, application (Level 3) data are used. In this case, those types of data were collected, but more important, business impact, ROI, and intangibles added to the rich database that influenced this critical decision. It is much less risky when a full implementation is recommended from a pilot program based on a full range of data.

Example 2: Global Financial Services

Global Financial Services conducted a program for relationship managers to teach them how to use software that would help them manage customer contacts. The program consisted of a one-day workshop, and 120 managers were trained on a pilot basis. Only sixty of the managers participating in the pilot were part of the evaluation project.

Payoff Measures

• Increased sales from existing customers

• Reduction in customer complaints

Key Intangibles

• Taking less time to respond to customers

• Customer satisfaction

Business Impact Measures

Value of increased sales to existing customers	$539,280
Value of reduced customer complaints	575,660
Total	$1,114,940

Program Costs

Development costs	$10,500
Materials and software	18,850
Equipment	6,000
Instructor (including expenses)	7,200
Facilities, food, and refreshments (60 @ $58)	3,480
Participants' time (salaries and benefits)	22,330
Coordination and evaluation	15,600
Total	$83,960

ROI Calculation

$$\text{ROI}(\%) = \frac{\$1,114,940 - \$83,960}{\$83,960} \times 100 = 1,228\%$$

Example 3: Healthcare, Inc.

Healthcare, Inc., conducted a one-day sexual harassment prevention workshop designed for all first- and second-level supervisors and managers. Seventeen sessions, involving 655 managers, took place over a period of forty-five days.

Payoff Measures

• Reduction in sexual harassment complaints

• Reduced turnover

Key Intangibles

- Job satisfaction

- Absenteeism

- Stress reduction

- Image of Healthcare, Inc.

- Recruiting

Business Impact Measures

Internal complaints	$360,276
Turnover reduction	2,840,632
Total	$3,200,908

Program Costs

Needs assessment (estimated cost of time)	$9,000
Program development and acquisition	15,000
Program coordination and facilitation time	9,600
Travel and lodging for facilitators and coordinators	1,520
Program materials (655 @ $12)	7,860
Food and refreshments (655 @ $30)	19,650
Facilities (17 @ $150)	2,550
Participant salaries and benefits ($130,797 × 1.39)	181,807
Evaluation	31,000
Total	$277,987

ROI Calculation

$$ROI(\%) = \frac{\$3,200,908 - \$277,987}{\$277,987} \times 100 = 1,052\%$$

Example 4: Metro Transit Authority

Metro Transit Authority conducted a program that initiated two processes: a no-fault disciplinary system was implemented, and the selection process for new drivers was modified. This program was implemented throughout the company, which employed 2,900 drivers.

Payoff Measure

• Reduced driver absenteeism

Key Intangible

• Improve customer service and satisfaction by reducing schedule delays caused by absenteeism

Business Impact Measures

Contribution of the no-fault policy	$518,000
Contribution of the new screening process	144,000
Total	$662,000

Program Costs

Cost of no-fault policy	
Development cost	$11,000
Materials	3,800
Meeting time	16,500
Total	$31,300
Cost of screening process	
Development cost	$20,000
Interviewer preparation	5,000
Administrative time (1,200 interviews × $7.25)	8,700
Materials (1,200 interviews × $2.00)	2,400
Total	$36,100

ROI Calculation

$$ROI(\%) = \frac{\$662,000 - \$67,400}{\$67,400} \times 100 = 882\%$$

Example 5: Midwest Electric

In a stress management program conducted by Midwest Electric, managers and representative employees participated in focus groups to identify work satisfiers and de-stressors and then collaborated on alleviating systemic sources of stress.

Payoff Measures

- Reduced medical care costs

- Reduced absenteeism

- Reduced turnover

Key Intangibles

- Improved communication

- Time savings

- Fewer conflicts

- Teamwork

- Improvement in problem solving

Business Impact Measures

Reduced medical costs	$198,720
Reduced absenteeism	67,684
Reduced turnover	157,553
Total	$423,957

Project Costs

Needs assessment	$16,500
Program development	4,800
Program materials (144 @ $95)	13,680
Participant salaries and benefits (based on 1 day)	24,108
Travel and lodging (144 @ $38)	5,472
Facilitation, coordination (including travel and overhead)	10,800
Meeting room, food, and refreshments (144 @ $22)	3,168
Evaluation costs	22,320
Total	$100,848

ROI Calculation

$$\text{ROI(\%)} = \frac{\$423{,}957 - \$100{,}848}{\$100{,}848} \times 100 = 320\%$$

Positioning ROI Evaluation

When ROI evaluation is undertaken, some important issues must be considered. This section presents information on how to position ROI measurement to harness the power of the ROI Methodology and the organizational resources that will support the process.

Choosing the Right Formula

What quantitative measure best represents top management goals? Many managers are preoccupied with the measures of sales, profits (net income), and profit percentages (the ratio of profits to dollar sales). However, the ultimate test of profitability is not the absolute amount of profit or the relationship of profit to sales. The critical test is the relationship of profit to invested capital. The most popular expression of this relationship is return on investment (Anthony and Reece, 1983).

Profits can be generated through increased sales or through cost savings. In practice, more opportunities are available for cost savings than for increased sales. Cost savings can be generated when productivity, quality, efficiency, cycle time, or actual cost reduction is improved. Among almost five hundred ROI studies that we have been involved in, the vast majority of the programs were based on cost savings. Approximately 85 percent of the studies had a payoff based on improvement of output, quality, or efficiency or on reduction of cost or time spent. The other studies had a payoff based on sales increases, in which benefits were derived from the profit margin. It is important for nonprofits and public sector organizations to take note of this situation. Because most performance improvement initiatives are aimed at cost savings, ROI evaluations can still be developed in those settings, even though the opportunity for profit is often unavailable.

In the finance and accounting literature, return on investment is defined as net income (earnings) divided by investment. In the context of performance improvement, net income is equivalent to net monetary benefits (program benefits minus program costs). Investment is equivalent to program costs. The term *investment* is used in three different senses in financial analysis, resulting in three different ROI ratios: return on assets (ROA), return on owners' equity (ROE), and return on capital employed (ROCE).

Financial executives have used ROI for centuries. Still, ROI did not become widespread in industry as a performance measure until the early 1960s. Conceptually, ROI has innate appeal because it blends all the major ingredients of profitability in one number; the ROI statistic by itself can be used to compare opportunities internally or externally. Practically, however, ROI should be used in conjunction with other performance measurements (Horngren, 1982).

The formula presented in this chapter should be the same formula that is used in the entire organization. Deviations from or misuse of the formula may create confusion among users or among the finance and accounting staff. Your chief financial officer (CFO) and your finance and accounting staff should be your partners in implementing the ROI Methodology. Without their support, involvement, and commitment, using the ROI Methodology on a wide-scale basis will be difficult. In recognition of this important relationship, the same financial terms used and expected by the CFO should be used when conducting and reporting the results of an evaluation.

Table 3.3 shows some common misuses of financial terms that appear in the literature. Terms such as *return on intelligence* (or *return on information*) abbreviated as ROI do nothing but confuse a CFO, who thinks that ROI is *return on investment*, as was described earlier. Sometimes, *return on expectations* (ROE), *return on*

Table 3.3. Misuse of Financial Terms

Term	Misuse	CFO Definition
ROI	Return on information	Return on investment
	Return on intelligence	
ROE	Return on expectation	Return on equity
ROA	Return on anticipation	Return on assets
ROCE	Return on client expectations	Return on capital employed
ROP	Return on people	??
ROR	Return on resources	??
ROT	Return on training	??
ROW	Return on Web	??

anticipation (ROA), or *return on client expectations* (ROCE) is used, also confusing the CFO, who thinks that those abbreviations stand for *return on equity, return on assets,* and *return on capital employed,* respectively. Use of misleading terms or abbreviations in calculating the payback of a program will confuse the finance and accounting staff and may cause them to withdraw their support from the evaluation project. Other terms such as *return on people, return on resources, return on training,* and *return on Web* are often used, with almost no consistent financial calculations. The bottom line: don't confuse the CFO. This individual (or her representative) should be considered an ally, and the same terminology, processes, and concepts used by her and her department should be used when describing the financial returns of programs.

Developing ROI Objectives

When reviewing the ROI calculation, it is helpful to position the ROI calculation in the context of all the data. The ROI calculation is only one measure generated with the ROI Methodology. Six types of data are developed and categorized along the five-level evaluation framework. The data collected at each level of evaluation are driven by a specific objective, as was described earlier

Figure 3.1. The Chain of Impact Drives ROI

Level	Objective	Results
1 Reaction and Planned Action	• Obtain a positive reaction to the program	• Average overall rating of 4.11 out of a possible 5
	• At least 75% of participants provide a list of action items	• 93% provided list of action items
2 Learning	• Knowledge of policy on sexual harassment; knowledge of inappropriate and illegal behavior	• Posttest scores averaged 84; pretest scores averaged 51 — improvement of 65% ([84–51]/51=65)
	• Skills to investigate and discuss sexual harassment	• Participants demonstrated that they could use the skills successfully
3 Application and Implementation	• Conduct meeting with employees	• 100% of participants conducted meetings with employees two weeks after the program
	• Administer policy to ensure that workplace is free from sexual harassment	• When confronted with a violation of policy, managers took appropriate action
	• Complete action items	• 80% of participants completed 3 out of 3 action items.
4 Business Impact	• Reduce the number of formal internal sexual harassment complaints	• Complaints reduced from 55 to 35
	• Reduce turnover related to sexual harassment	• Turnover reduced from 24.2% to 19.9%
	• Reduce absenteeism related to sexual harass-ment	• Increased job satisfaction • Increased teamwork • Reduced stress
5 ROI	• Obtain at least a 25% ROI	• ROI = 1052%

in this series. Specific objectives are often set for ROI, creating expectations about an acceptable ROI value.

Figure 3.1 shows the payoff of a program to prevent sexual harassment. The results at the different levels are clearly linked to the specific objectives of the program. As objectives are established, data are collected to indicate the extent to which the objectives were met. This framework clearly shows the powerful connection between objectives, measurement, and evaluation data. The table also shows the chain of impact: reaction leads to learning, which leads to application, which leads to business impact and to ROI. The intangible benefits shown in the business impact category are items that were purposely not converted to monetary values. Some of those outcomes could have been anticipated before the program was implemented. Others may not have been anticipated but were described as a benefit by those involved in the program. In this example, an ROI of 25 percent was expected. This organization uses 25 percent as a standard for all programs slated for an ROI evaluation. The result of 1,052 percent clearly exceeded that objective by a huge amount.

Determining ROI Targets

Specific expectations for ROI should be developed before an evaluation study is undertaken. While there are no generally accepted standards, *ROI Fundamentals*, the first book of this series, discusses four strategies for setting ROI targets:

- Setting the goal at the same level as other capital investments

- Setting the target at a higher level than other investments

- Aiming for a 0% ROI—that is, breaking even

- Letting the client set the ROI target

This issue should always be addressed before a program begins.

Other ROI Measures

In addition to the traditional ROI and BCR formulas described earlier in this chapter, several other measures are occasionally used to evaluate return on investment in a broad sense. These measures are designed primarily to evaluate other types of financial investments but sometimes work their way into program evaluations.

Payback Period

The payback period is a common method of evaluating capital expenditures. In this approach, the original cash outlay is divided by the annual cash proceeds (savings) produced by that investment to arrive at some multiple of cash proceeds that is equal to the original investment. Measurement is usually in terms of years and months. For example, if the cost savings generated by a program are constant each year, the payback period is determined by dividing the total original cash investment (development costs, outside program purchases, and so on) by the amount of the expected or actual annual savings.

To practice this calculation, assume that a program's cost is $100,000 and that the program has a three-year useful life. The annual net savings from the program are expected to be $40,000. The payback period is as follows:

$$\text{Payback period} = \frac{\text{Total Investment}}{\text{Annual Savings}} = \frac{\$100,000}{\$40,000} = 2.5 \text{ years}$$

The program will "pay back" the original investment in 2.5 years.

Payback period is a simple concept to use, but it has the limitation of ignoring the time value of money. It has not enjoyed widespread use in evaluating program investments.

Exhibit 3.2 compares BCR, ROI, and payback period for the same program. These calculations are obviously related, and sometimes, all three are reported because of the different perspectives they provide. The payback period figure answers the question "How long will it take to get the investment back (or break even, or achieve a 0% ROI)?" Sometimes, this is referred to as a *break-even analysis*.

Discounted Cash Flow

Discounted cash flow is a method of evaluating investment opportunities in which values assigned are based on the timing of the

Exhibit 3.2. Comparison of ROI, BCR, and Payback Period

Defining Benefit-Cost Ratio

$$BCR = \frac{\text{Program Benefits}}{\text{Program Costs}}$$

Example

Program Benefits = $71,760
Program Costs = $32,984

$$BCR = \frac{\$71,760}{\$32,984} = 2.18$$

Defining Return on Investment

$$ROI(\%) = \frac{\text{Net Program Benefits}}{\text{Program Costs}} \times 100$$

Example

Net Program Benefits = $38,776
Program Costs = $32,984

$$ROI(\%) = \frac{\$38,776}{\$32,984} \times 100 = 118\%$$

Defining Payback Period

$$\text{Payback Period} = \frac{\text{Total Investment}}{\text{Annual Savings}} \times 12$$

Example

Total Investment = $32,984
Annual Savings = $71,760

$$\text{Payback Period} = \frac{\$32,984}{\$71,760} = .46 \times 12 = 5.52 \text{ months}$$

proceeds from the investment. The assumption, based on interest rates, is that money earned today is more valuable than money earned a year from now. Discounted cash flow is used when it is important to understand the value of future returns.

There are several ways of using the concept of discounted cash flow to evaluate capital expenditures. The most popular is probably the net present value of an investment. This approach compares the savings, year by year, with the outflow of cash required by the investment. The expected savings for each year is discounted by a selected interest rate. The outflow of cash is also discounted by the same interest rate. If the present value of all the savings is expected to exceed the present value of all the outlays after discounting at a common interest rate, the investment is usually acceptable in the eyes of management. The discounted cash flow method has the advantage of allowing managers to rank investments, but it can be difficult to calculate.

Internal Rate of Return

The internal rate of return (IRR) method determines the interest rate required to make the present value of the cash flow equal to zero. It represents the maximum rate of interest that could be paid if all program funds were borrowed and the organization had to break even on the programs. The IRR considers the time value of money and is unaffected by the scale of the program. It can be used to rank alternatives and to make accept-or-reject decisions when a minimum rate of return is specified. A major weakness of the IRR method is that it assumes that all returns are reinvested at the same internal rate of return. This can make an investment alternative with a high rate of return look even better than it really is, and a program with a low rate of return may look even worse. In practice, the IRR is rarely used to evaluate program investments.

Utility Analysis

An interesting approach to calculating the payoff of a program is utility analysis. Utility analysis measures the economic contribution of a program according to how effective the program was in identifying and modifying behavior and, hence, the future service contribution of employees. Utility is a function of the duration of a program's effect on employees' performance, the number of employees involved, the validity of the program, the value of the job for which the program was provided, and the total program cost (Schmidt, Hunter, and Pearlman, 1982). The following formula is offered for assessing the dollar value of a program:

$$\Delta U = T \times N \times dt \times SDy - N \times C$$

where

$\Delta U =$ Monetary value of the program

$T =$ Duration of a program's effect on performance, in years

$N =$ Number of employees involved

$dt =$ True difference in average job performance between employees in the program and those not in the program, in units of standard deviation

$SDy =$ Standard deviation of job performance of those not involved in the program, in dollars

$C =$ Cost of the program per employee

Of all the factors in this formula, the true difference in job performance (dt) and the value of the target job (SDy) are the most difficult to place a value on. The validity of the program (dt) is determined by noting the performance differences between employees participating in the program and those not participating. The simplest way to obtain this information is to have supervisors rate the performance of each group. Supervisors and experts can estimate the value of the target job (SDy).

Utility analysis has advantages and disadvantages. It has two primary flaws. First, it is basically a Level 3 ROI analysis. Essentially, the process converts behavior change (Level 3) into monetary value, ignoring the consequences of that behavior change, which is the business impact (Level 4). As a result, it stops short of following the chain of impact all the way to the new behavior's consequences within the organization. Simply having new behavior in place does not mean that it is being used productively or adding value to the organization.

The second disadvantage is that utility analysis is based on estimates. Because of the subjective nature of estimates and many managers' reluctance to use them, the process has not achieved widespread acceptance among professionals as a practical tool for evaluating return on investment. A recent survey of two hundred published case studies on ROI found that less than 5 percent use utility analysis.

One possible advantage is that researchers have developed an abundance of models. One of the principal proponents of the process identifies six models that use the concept of utility analysis (Cascio, 2000).

Also, the notion of putting a value on behavior change is a novel idea for many practitioners. Given the increased interest in leadership behaviors and job competencies, the prospect of placing a value on those behaviors in the workplace has some appeal and explains the application of utility analysis in some situations. For example, the Eastman Chemical Company used this process to evaluate an empowerment program for employees (Bernthal and Byham, 1997).

Utility analysis should be one of the tools in a manager's ROI arsenal. In the framework presented in this series of books, utility analysis is a Level 3 ROI analysis, which, in essence, forecasts the value or impact of a program based on behavior change.

ROI, the Profit Center, and EVA

Given increased interest in converting various organizational functions to profit centers, distinguishing between the ROI Methodology and the profit center strategy is important. The ROI Methodology described in this series of books shows the payoff of a program (or a group of programs) with highly integrated objectives. It is a microlevel process showing the economic value derived from these programs. The profit center concept usually applies to an entire function, which operates like a privately owned business, with profit as the true measure of its economic success. Its customers, usually the key managers in the organization, have complete discretion on whether to use the internal services of the function or to purchase those services externally. When the services are purchased internally, competitive prices are usually charged and transferred from the operating department, providing revenue to the function. The function's expenses include salaries, office space, materials, fees, and services. Thus, the function operates as a wholly owned subsidiary of the organization, receiving revenues for all services provided and paying out expenses for its staff and operations. The function realizes a profit if the revenue received from the transfer of funds exceeds the costs. This approach holds much interest, particularly for senior executives who want to bring complete accountability to their organization's functions. Also, the profit center approach provides a true test of the perceived value of an organizational function when managers have complete autonomy in their decisions to use each function's services or not.

The profit center concept can be seen as a higher level of evaluation, as depicted in Figure 3.2, which shows the progression of

Figure 3.2. Relationship of the Profit Center to the Evaluation Levels of the ROI Methodology

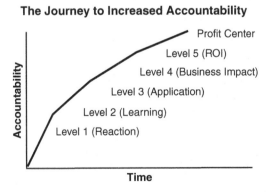

evaluation levels, including the profit center. Level 1 has been used for many years and represents the most common and accepted evaluation data. Level 2 followed, as did Levels 3, 4, and 5. The profit center concept is a higher level of accountability, if it can be achieved. In essence, this level of measurement places a value on the entire function and can show its economic value added (EVA) to the organization. This concept is particularly important because of recent emphasis on economic value added (Young and O'Byrne, 2001). This concept can be applied to functions that generate revenue to offset expenses.

Figure 3.2 also underscores the fact that the previous levels of evaluation must be in place in order for the next level to work. If Level 4 and 5 evaluations have not become a routine part of the measurement scheme, running an effective profit center will be difficult. Some organizations that have failed in the move to the profit center arrangement relied on their success with Level 1 and 2 evaluations, skipping Levels 3, 4, and 5. Because participants reacted positively or developed skills, the program staff perceived that the programs were adding value. Operating managers, on the other hand, were unable to recognize this value, and were reluctant to purchase the programs, when given an option. They were not convinced of the added value because they had not seen any previous data that showed the impact of the programs in their operating departments.

The profit center and EVA are excellent concepts for evaluating the impact of an entire organizational function. Using these concepts is a goal of many executives and managers. In reality, there are many barriers to making the process operational. Not every program should be optional; some programs are necessary. In addition, some programs and initiatives need to be consistent, so their quality needs to be controlled in some way. Allowing managers to opt out of programs and purchase their own may cause them to develop a wide variety of programs that do not necessarily add value. Still, many managers have made the establishment of profit centers one of their goals.

Final Thoughts

This chapter has shown the different ways in which ROI can be calculated, as well as some of the basic interpretations of those calculations. It has also shown the relationships between the different methods of calculation. The ROI formula and the benefit-cost ratio are emphasized because these are the two principal ways in which Level 5 ROI is expressed. The next chapter covers some basic issues involved in ROI calculation.

References

Anthony, R., and Reece, J. *Accounting: Text and Cases.* (7th ed.) Homewood, Ill.: Irwin, 1983.

Bernthal, P., and Byham, B. "Evaluation of Techniques for an Empowered Workforce." In J. J. Phillips (ed.), *In Action: Measuring Return on Investment,* Vol. 2. Alexandria, Va.: American Society for Training and Development, 1997.

Cascio, W. *Costing Human Resources: The Financial Impact of Behavior in Organizations.* London: South-Western College Pub and Thomson Learning, 2000.

Horngren, C. *Cost Accounting.* (5th ed.) Englewood Cliffs, N.J.: Prentice-Hall, 1982.

Schmidt, F., Hunter, J., and Pearlman, K. "Assessing the Economic Impact of Personnel Programs on Workforce Productivity." *Personnel Psychology,* 1982, 35, 333–347.

Seagraves, T. "Mission Possible: Selling Complex Services over the Phone." In J. J. Phillips (ed.), *In Action: Measuring Return on Investment,* Vol. 3. Alexandria, Va.: American Society for Training and Development, 2001.

Young, S., and O'Byrne, S. *EVA® and Value-Based Management: A Practical Guide to Implementation.* New York: McGraw-Hill, 2001.

4

ROI Issues

This chapter describes some of the basic issues involved in the use of the ROI Methodology. Some of these issues have been covered in other books, but they are summarized and integrated here in a thorough discussion of the use of ROI, emphasizing its advantages and disadvantages and some of the concerns that arise at this level of accountability.

ROI Can Be Very Large

As the examples in this book have demonstrated, the actual ROI value can be quite large, far exceeding what might be expected from other types of investments in plants, equipment, and companies. Programs for leadership, team building, management development, supervisor training, and sales training can generate ROIs in the 100 percent to 700 percent range. This does not mean that all ROI studies result in a positive ROI; many ROIs are negative. However, the impact of programs can be quite impressive. It is helpful to remember what constitutes the ROI value. For example, the investment in a one-week program for a team leader could generate an impressive ROI. If the leader's behavior changes as he works directly with his team, a chain of impact might produce a measurable change in performance from the team. That behavior change, translated into a measurement improvement for the entire

Figure 4.1. Factors That Contribute to High ROI Values

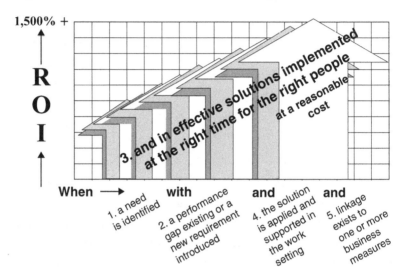

year, might be quite significant. When the monetary value of the team's improvement is considered for an entire year and compared with the relatively small amount of investment in one team leader, it is easy to see why this number can be quite large.

More specifically, as Figure 4.1 shows, some important factors contribute to high ROI values. The impact can be large when a specific need has been identified and a performance gap exists; a new requirement is introduced and the solution is implemented at the right time for the right people at a reasonable cost; the solution is applied and supported in the work setting; and the solution is linked to one or more business measures. When these conditions are met, high ROI values can be achieved.

It is important to understand that a very high ROI can occur and not necessarily relate directly to the health of the rest of the organization. For example, a high-impact ROI can be generated in an organization that is losing money (or in bankruptcy) because the impact is restricted to the individuals involved in the program and the monetary value of their improvement is connected to that program. At the same time, a disastrous program can generate a very negative ROI in a company that is profitable. ROI evaluations are microlevel activities that evaluate the success of one program within a particular time frame.

What Happens When the ROI Is Negative?

Perhaps one of the greatest fears in using ROI is the possibility of having a negative ROI. This fear concerns not only the program sponsor or owner but also those who are involved in the design, development, and delivery of the program. Few individuals want to be involved in a process that exposes a failure. Those who are involved will naturally be concerned that failure may reflect unfavorably on them.

On the positive side, a negative ROI provides the best opportunity for learning (process improvement). The ROI Methodology reveals problems and barriers. As data are collected throughout the chain of impact, the reasons for failure become clear. Data on barriers and enablers to the transfer of skills captured at Level 3 (Application) usually reveal why the program did not work.

While a negative result from an ROI evaluation is the ultimate learning situation, no one wants to invite that opportunity to his or her door. The preference is to learn from others! Sometimes the damage created by a negative ROI is the sense of expectations that were not managed properly up front and fear of the consequences of the negative ROI. The following steps can help minimize or avoid this dilemma.

1. Raise questions about the feasibility of an impact study: Is it appropriate to use the ROI Methodology for this particular program? Sometimes, a program by its very nature may appear to be a failure, at least in terms of ROI.

2. Make sure that all interested parties have a clear understanding of the consequences of a negative ROI. This issue should be addressed early and often. The ROI Methodology is a process improvement tool, not a performance evaluation tool. No one

wants to be involved in a process that may reflect unfavorably on his or her performance. The individuals involved should not necessarily be penalized or have their performance evaluated unfavorably because of a negative ROI.

3. Look for warning signs early in the process; they are usually everywhere. Level 1 data often send strong signals that an evaluation may result in a negative ROI. Some signals of a potential negative ROI may be that the participants react negatively, do not see the relevance of the program to their jobs, perceive the content to be inappropriate, consider the information outdated, offer no intent to use the material, or refuse to recommend the program to anyone else.

4. Manage expectations. Lower expectations about the ROI are better. Anticipating a high ROI and communicating that prospect to the client or other stakeholders may create an expectation that might not materialize. Keep expectations low and the delivery performance high.

5. Use negative data to reposition the story. Rather than communicating that great results have been achieved with a very effective program, the story becomes, "We have some great information that tells us how to change the program to obtain better results." This story line is more than a nice turn of phrase; it underscores the importance of learning what went wrong and what can be done in the future to positively affect the ROI.

6. Use the information to drive change. Sometimes, the negative ROI can be transformed into a positive ROI with some minor alterations of the program. Implementation issues—for example, providing more support for the use of knowledge and skills in the workplace—may need to be addressed. In other situations, a complete redesign of the program may be necessary. In a few isolated cases, discontinuing the program may be the only option. Whatever the option, use the data to drive action so that the overall value of conducting the study has been realized.

These strategies can help minimize the unfavorable and some-times disastrous perceptions that can result from a negative ROI.

ROI Is Not for Every Program

The ROI Methodology should not be applied to every program. It takes time and resources to create a valid and credible ROI study. Although this issue is addressed in other books in this series, under-scoring the types of programs for which this technique is best suited is appropriate at this stage. ROI is appropriate for programs that

- Have a long life cycle; at some point in the life of the program, this level of accountability should be applied to the program.

- Are important to the organization in meeting its opera-tional goals; these programs are designed to add value, and ROI may be helpful in showing that value.

- Are closely linked to the organization's strategic initia-tives; anything this important needs a high level of accountability.

- Are expensive to implement; an expensive program that deploys large amounts of resources should be subjected to this level of accountability.

- Are highly visible and sometimes controversial; these programs often require this level of accountability in order to satisfy the critics.

- Have a large target audience; if a program is designed for all employees, it may be a candidate for ROI.

- Command the interest of the top executive group; if top executives are interested in knowing the impact, the ROI Methodology should be applied.

These are only guidelines and should be considered in the context of the organization in which they are being applied. Other criteria may also be appropriate. Criteria can be prioritized in a scheme to identify the programs most appropriate for this level of accountability.

It is also helpful to consider the type of programs for which the ROI Methodology is not appropriate. ROI is seldom appropriate for programs that

- Are very short in duration, such as two-hour briefings; changing behavior in such a short time frame is difficult.

- Are legislated or required by regulation; changing anything as a result of an evaluation might be difficult if the program is obligatory, legally mandated, or regulated.

- Are required by senior management; it may be that these programs will continue regardless of the findings.

- Serve as operator training and technical skills development; it may be more appropriate to measure at Levels 1, 2, and 3 to ensure that participants know how to do the job and are doing it properly.

These guidelines do not imply that the ROI Methodology cannot be implemented for these types of programs. However, careful use of limited resources and time for measurement and evaluation will result in evaluating more strategic programs. It is also helpful to think about what kind of programs are appropriate for an organization's first one or two ROI studies. Initially, the use of this process will be met with some anxiety and tentativeness. The programs initially evaluated should not only meet the requirements listed earlier but should also meet other requirements. These programs should

- Be as simple as possible; reserve the complex programs for later.

- Be a known commodity, with the perception of positive results; this will help to ensure that the first study does not have a negative result.

- Be free of hidden agendas and political sensitivity; the first study should not be caught up in the organization's politics.

Deciding the level at which to allocate resources to the process of ROI evaluation, which programs to evaluate for ROI, and the number of programs to pursue in any given time frame are important issues.

Concerns About ROI

Following are some cautions to observe when you are evaluating ROI, as well as a discussion of myths that practitioners may struggle with as they begin to assess ROI in their programs.

Cautions

Caution is needed when developing, calculating, and communicating ROI. The implementation of the ROI Methodology is a very important issue and a goal of many managers and professionals. In addition to the guiding principles, a few issues should be addressed to keep the process from going astray. The following cautions are offered to aid you in evaluating ROI.

Take a Conservative Approach When Developing Benefits and Costs

Conservatism in an ROI evaluation builds accuracy and credibility. What matters most is how the target audience perceives the value of the data. A conservative approach is always recommended for both the numerator of the ROI formula (benefits) and the denominator (program costs). A conservative approach is the basis for the Guiding Principles that are described throughout this series.

Make Sure That ROI of Programs Is Not Confused with Other Financial Measures of Return

The return on funds invested or assets employed can be calculated in many ways. ROI is just one of them. Although the calculation for the ROI of programs and projects uses the same basic formula as the formula used for the ROI for capital investment evaluations, it may not be fully understood by the target audience. Its calculation method and its meaning should be clearly communicated. More important, it should be accepted by management as an appropriate measure for program evaluation.

Involve Management in Calculating ROI

Management ultimately decides whether an ROI value is acceptable. To the extent possible, management should be involved in setting the parameters for calculations and establishing the targets for determining whether programs are acceptable within the organization.

Fully Disclose Assumptions and Methodology

When you are discussing the ROI Methodology and communicating data, fully disclosing the process, steps, and assumptions used in the process is very important. Strengths should be clearly communicated as well as weaknesses and shortcomings.

Approach Sensitive and Controversial Issues with Caution

Occasionally, sensitive and controversial issues will be raised during a discussion of an ROI value. It is best to avoid debates over what is measurable and what is not measurable unless clear evidence on the issue in question is available. Also, some programs are so fundamental to the survival of an organization that measuring them is unnecessary. For example, a program designed to improve customer service in a customer-focused company may escape the scrutiny of an ROI evaluation based on the assumption that if the program is well designed, it will improve customer service.

Teach Others the Methods for Calculating ROI

Each time an ROI is calculated, there is an opportunity to educate other managers and colleagues within the organization. Even if they are not responsible for the program, these individuals will be able to see the value of this approach to program evaluation. Also, when possible, each project should serve as a case study in order to educate the staff on specific techniques and methods.

Recognize That Not Everyone Will Buy into ROI

Not every audience member will understand, appreciate, or accept the ROI calculation. For a variety of reasons, one or more individuals may not agree with the values. These individuals may be highly emotional about the concept of showing accountability for specific types of programs. Attempts to persuade them may be beyond the scope of the task at hand. This may be a long-term program, and you may need to use some of the techniques presented in *Communication and Implementation*, book six of this series, to persuade these members of your audience.

Do Not Boast About a High Return

It is not unusual for a high-impact program to generate a high ROI. Several examples in this book have illustrated such possibilities.

An evaluator who boasts about a high rate of return will be open to criticism from others unless the calculation is based on indisputable facts.

Choose the Place for Debates

The time to debate the ROI Methodology is not during a presentation (unless it can't be avoided). Choose appropriate situations in which to constructively debate the ROI Methodology: in a special forum, among staff, in an educational session, in professional literature, on panel discussions, or even during the development of an ROI impact study. The time and place for debate should be carefully selected so as not to detract from the quality and quantity of information presented.

Use ROI to Evaluate Selected Programs

As we discussed earlier, some programs are difficult to quantify and for those, an ROI calculation may not be feasible. Other methods of presenting the benefits may be more appropriate. Targets should be set for the percentage of programs in which ROI will be assessed. Also, specific criteria should be established in order to select programs for ROI analysis.

ROI Myths

Although most practitioners recognize the ROI Methodology as an important addition to measurement and evaluation, they often struggle with how to address the issue. Many professionals see the ROI Methodology as a ticket to increased funding and prosperity for programs. They believe that without it, they may be lost in the shuffle, and with it, they may gain the respect they need to continue moving their department or function forward. Regardless of their motivation for pursuing ROI evaluation, the key questions are "Is it a feasible process that can be implemented with reasonable resources?" and "Will it provide the benefits necessary to make it a useful, sustainable tool?" The answer to these questions may lead to debate and even controversy.

The controversy surrounding the ROI Methodology stems from misunderstandings about what it can and cannot do and how it can or should be implemented within an organization. To conclude this chapter, these misunderstandings are summarized as myths about the ROI Methodology. The myths are based on years of experience with ROI evaluation and the perceptions observed during hundreds of studies and workshops conducted by the ROI Institute. Along with each myth, we present an appropriate explanation.

ROI Is Too Complex for Most Users

This myth is a problem because of a few highly complex ROI models that have been publicly presented. Unfortunately, these models have done little to help users and have caused confusion about ROI. The ROI Methodology is a basic financial formula for accountability that is simple and understandable: earnings are divided by investment; earnings are the net benefits from a program, and the investment equals the total cost of the program. Straying from this basic formula can add confusion and create tremendous misunderstanding. The ROI model provides a step-by-step, systematic process. Each step is taken separately, and issues are addressed for that particular step; the decisions are made incrementally throughout the process. This method helps reduce a complex process to simple, manageable efforts.

ROI Is Expensive, Consuming Too Many Critical Resources

The ROI Methodology can become expensive if it is not carefully organized, controlled, and implemented. While the cost of an external ROI evaluation can be significant, many actions can be taken to keep costs down. Ways to save costs when evaluating ROI are presented in *Communication and Implementation*, book six of this series.

If Senior Management Does Not Require ROI, There Is No Need to Pursue It

This myth affects the most innocent bystanders. It is easy to be lulled into providing measurement and evaluation that simply preserves the status quo, believing that no pressure or request for ROI means no requirement. The truth is that if senior executives have seen only Level 1 reaction data, they may not be asking for higher-level data because they think that those types of data are not available. In some cases, leaders have convinced top management that their programs cannot be evaluated at the ROI level or that the specific impact of some types of programs cannot be determined. Given these conditions, it comes as no surprise that some top managers are not asking for ROI data.

There is another problem with the laid-back approach. Paradigms are shifting. Senior managers are beginning to request this level of data more and more often. Changes in corporate leadership sometimes initiate important paradigm shifts. New leaders often require higher levels of accountability for current and future programs. The process of integrating the ROI Methodology into an organization takes time—about twelve to eighteen months in many organizations; it is not a quick fix. However, when senior executives suddenly ask for ROI measurement, they may expect results to be produced quickly. Because this type of sudden request could occur at any time, proactive leaders will initiate implementation of the ROI Methodology and begin to develop ROI evaluations long before senior management asks for ROI data.

ROI Is a Passing Fad

Unfortunately, many of the processes being introduced in organizations today are indeed fads. However, the need to account for expenditures will always be present, and the ROI Methodology provides the ultimate level of accountability. ROI has been used for years to measure the investment of equipment and new manufacturing plants. Now, it is being used in many other areas, for all types of programs and projects. Drawing on its rich history, evaluators will continue to use ROI as an important tool in measurement and evaluation, extending it into other applications.

ROI Is Only One Type of Data

This is a common misunderstanding. The ROI calculation represents one type of data that shows the benefits versus the costs of a program. However, when the complete five-level evaluation framework is used, six types of data are generated, representing both qualitative and quantitative data and, often, data from different sources, making the ROI Methodology a rich source for a variety of data.

ROI Is Not Future-Oriented; It Reflects Only Past Performance

Unfortunately, many evaluation processes are past-oriented and reflect only what has already happened in a program; this is the only way to accurately assess impact. However, the ROI Methodology can easily be adapted to forecast ROI, as the next chapter describes.

ROI Is Rarely Used by Organizations

This myth is easily dispelled when the evidence is fully examined. More than 3,000 organizations use the ROI Methodology, and more than two hundred case studies on the ROI Methodology have been published. Leading organizations throughout the world, including businesses of all sizes and sectors, use the ROI Methodology to increase accountability and improve programs. This process is also being used in the nonprofit, educational, and government sectors. There is no doubt that it is a widely used process that is growing in use.

The ROI Methodology Cannot Be Easily Replicated

This is an understandable concern. In theory, any process worthy of implementation is one that can be replicated from one study to another. For example, if two different people conducted an ROI evaluation on the same program, would they obtain the same results? Fortunately, the ROI Methodology is a systematic process with standards and guiding principles; the likelihood of two evaluators obtaining the same results is high. And because it is a process that involves step-by-step procedures, the ROI Methodology can also be replicated from one program to another.

The ROI Methodology Is Not a Credible Process; It Is Too Subjective

This myth has evolved because some ROI studies involving estimates have been promoted in the literature and at conferences. Many ROI studies have been conducted without the use of estimates. Estimates are often used when evaluators are attempting to isolate the effects of a program. Using estimates from the participants is only one of several techniques that can be used to isolate the effects of a program. Other techniques involve analytical approaches such as the use of control groups and trend line analysis. Sometimes, estimating is used in other steps of the ROI process, such as converting data to monetary values or estimating output in the data collection phase. In each of these situations, other options are often available, but for reasons of convenience or economics, estimation is often used. While the use of estimates often represents the least ideal scenario in the ROI Methodology, estimates can be extremely reliable when they are obtained carefully, adjusted for error, and reported appropriately. Practitioners in the fields of accounting, engineering, and technology routinely use estimates, often without question or concern.

ROI Cannot Be Evaluated for Soft-Skill Programs; It Is Only for Production and Sales

ROI measurement is often most effective in soft-skill programs, such as those in leadership development, culture, customer satisfaction, and employee engagement. Programs in soft skills such as learning often drive hard data items such as output, quality, cost, or time. Case after case shows successful application of the ROI Methodology in programs on such topics as team building, executive development, communications, and empowerment. Additional examples of successful ROI applications can be found in compliance programs in areas such as diversity, prevention of sexual harassment, and policy implementation.

Any type of program or process can be evaluated at the ROI level. Problems may surface when ROI is calculated for programs that should not be evaluated at this level. The ROI Methodology should be reserved for programs that are expensive, that address operational problems or issues related to strategic objectives, or that attract the interest of management because increased accountability is desired.

ROI Is Only for Manufacturing and Service Organizations

Although initial studies on ROI appeared in the manufacturing sector, the service sector quickly picked up the ROI process as a useful tool. After that, use of the ROI Methodology migrated to the nonprofit sector, and organizations such as hospitals and health care firms began endorsing and using the process. Next, ROI evaluation moved through the government sector around the world, and now, educational institutions are beginning to use the ROI Methodology. Several educational institutions use ROI evaluation to measure the impact of their formal degree programs and less-structured continuing education programs and community outreach programs.

It Is Not Always Possible to Isolate the Effects of a Program

Distinguishing the effects of a program from the effects of factors outside the program is always achievable when using the ROI Methodology. There are many ways to isolate the influence of a program, and at least one method will work in any given situation.

The challenge is selecting an appropriate isolation method for the resources and accuracy needed in a particular situation. This myth probably stems from unsuccessful attempts at using a control group arrangement—a classic way to isolate the effect of a process, program, or initiative. In practice, a control group approach does not work in a majority of situations, causing some researchers to abandon the issue of isolating program effects. In reality, many other techniques provide accurate, reliable, and valid methods for isolating the effects of a program.

Measurement of On-the-Job Activities Is Impossible Because Post-Program Control of Participants Is Impossible

This myth is fading as organizations face the reality of implementing workplace solutions to key problems and realize the importance of measuring on-the-job results. Although the program staff does not have direct control of what happens in the workplace, it can influence the process. A new program must be considered within the context of the workplace; the program is owned by the organization, even though individuals and groups involved in the program may have objectives that extend beyond work. Thus, program objectives focus on application and business impact data used in the ROI analysis. Ideally, partnership between key managers produces the objectives that drive the program. In effect, a program or project is a process with partnerships and a common framework to drive business results—not just classroom activity.

ROI Is Appropriate Only for Large Organizations

While it is true that large organizations with enormous budgets have the most interest in ROI, smaller organizations can also use the process, particularly when it is simplified and built into their programs. Organizations with as few as fifty employees have successfully applied the ROI Methodology, using it as a tool for increasing accountability and employee involvement.

The ROI Methodology Has No Standards

An important problem facing measurement and evaluation is a lack of standardization or consistency. Frequently asked questions include "What is a good ROI?" "What should be included in the cost so that I can compare my data with other data?" and "When should specific data be included in the ROI value instead of being left as an intangible benefit?" While these questions are not easily answered, some help is on the way. Standards for the ROI Methodology—the Guiding Principles—have been developed, and more details are also being developed. Also under development is a database that will share thousands of studies so that best practices, patterns, trends, and standards are readily available. For more information on these issues, visit www.roiinstitute.net.

Final Thoughts

The ROI Methodology is not for every organization, individual, or program. Use of the ROI Methodology represents a tremendous paradigm shift as organizations attempt to bring more accountability and results to a variety of programs and processes. The ROI Methodology brings a results-based approach and is client-focused, requiring much contact, communication, dialogue, and agreement with the client group. Key issues must be addressed in ROI calculations, and those issues are explored in this chapter. Cautions and myths about the ROI process are also discussed. The next chapter explains how to use the ROI Methodology to forecast a program's ROI.

5

ROI Forecasting

S ometimes, confusion arises about when evaluating ROI is appropriate. The traditional approach, described in this series, is to base ROI calculations strictly on business impact data obtained after the program has been implemented. In this approach, business performance measures (Level 4 data) are easily converted to a monetary value, which is necessary for an ROI calculation. This chapter shows that ROI calculations are possible in a variety of time frames, using a variety of data. Pre-program ROI forecasts are possible, as well as forecasts with reaction data (Level 1), learning data (Level 2), and application data (Level 3).

The Trade-Offs of Forecasting

ROI can be developed at different times, using different levels of data. Unfortunately, however, the ease, convenience, and low cost of capturing a forecasted ROI create trade-offs in accuracy and credibility. As Figure 5.1 illustrates, ROI can be evaluated at five distinct time intervals during the life cycle of a program. The relationships between credibility, accuracy, cost, and difficulty are also shown in the figure.

Here are descriptions of the five time intervals:

1. A pre-program forecast can be developed, using estimates of the impact of the program. This approach lacks credibility and

Figure 5.1. ROI Forecasts at Different Times and Levels

ROI with:	Data Collection Timing	Credibility	Accuracy	Cost to Develop	Difficulty
1. Pre-program data	Before program	Not very credible	Not very accurate	Inexpensive	Not difficult
2. Reaction and planned action data	Duriing program				
3. Learning data	During program				
4. Application and implementation data	After program				
5. Business impact data	After program	Very credible	Very accurate	Expensive	Very difficult

accuracy, but it is also the least expensive and least difficult ROI to calculate. There is value in developing the ROI on a pre-program basis. This will be discussed in the next section.

2. Reaction data can be extended in order to anticipate the impact of a program, including the ROI. In this case, participants anticipate the chain of impact as a program is applied and implemented and then influences specific business measures. While the accuracy and credibility are usually greater than those of the pre-program forecast, this approach still lacks the credibility and accuracy desired in most situations.

3. For some programs, learning data can be used to forecast the actual ROI. This approach is applicable only when formal testing shows a relationship between acquiring certain skills or knowledge and subsequent business performance. When this correlation is available (it is usually developed to validate the test that documents learning), test data can be used to forecast subsequent performance. The performance can then be converted to monetary impact, and the ROI can be developed. This technique has limited potential as an evaluation tool because only a few predictive validation studies have been developed.

4. In some situations, when actual use of skills is critical, the application and implementation of those skills or knowledge can be converted to a value, using employee compensation as a basis. This is particularly helpful in situations in which competencies are being developed and values are placed on improving competencies, even if there is no immediate increase in pay.

5. Finally, the ROI can be developed from business impact data converted directly to monetary values and compared with the costs of the program. This post-program evaluation is the basis for the other ROI calculations in this book and has been the principal approach used in previous chapters. It is the preferred approach, but because of the pressures outlined earlier, it is critical to examine ROI calculations in other time frames.

This chapter will discuss pre-program evaluation and the ROI calculations based on reactions in detail. ROI calculations developed from learning and application data will be discussed more briefly. Examples will illustrate the process.

Pre-Program ROI Forecasting

Perhaps one of the most useful steps in convincing a sponsor that an expense is appropriate is to forecast the ROI for the program. The process is similar to post-program analysis, except that the extent of the impact must be estimated along with the forecasted cost.

Basic Model

Figure 5.2 shows the basic model for capturing the data necessary for a pre-program forecast; this model is a modified version of the post-program ROI process model presented in *ROI Fundamentals*, the first book in this series. In the pre-program forecast, the program outcomes are estimated before program implementation rather than collected after program implementation. Data collection is kept simple, relying on interviews, focus groups, or surveys of experts. Tapping into benchmarking studies or locating previous studies may also be helpful.

Beginning at the reaction level, anticipated or estimated reactions are captured. Next, the anticipated learning is developed, followed by the anticipated application and implementation data. Here, the estimates focus on what must be accomplished in order for the program to be successful. These items may be based on the objectives at each of these levels. Finally, the impact data are estimated by experts. These experts may include subject matter experts, the program supplier, or potential participants in the program. In this model, the levels build on each other. Estimating data at Levels 1, 2, and 3 enhances the quality of the estimated data at Level 4 (impact), which is needed for the analysis.

Figure 5.2. Pre-Program Forecasting Model

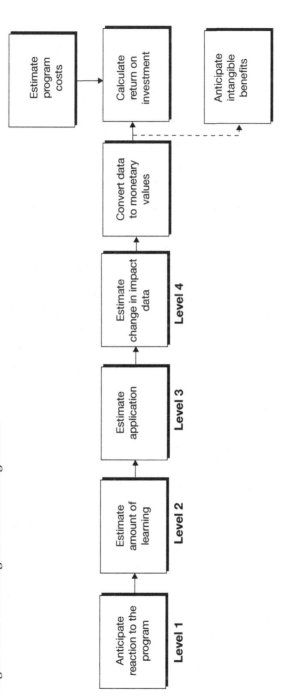

The model shows that there is no need to isolate the effects of a program as in the post-program model. The individual providing the data is asked the following question: "How much will the business impact measure change as a result of the program?" This question ties the change in the measure directly to the program; thus, isolation is not needed. This approach makes the pre-program process of estimating ROI easier than the post-program ROI process, in which isolating program impact is always required.

Converting data to a monetary value is straightforward; a limited number of techniques are available for data conversion. Locating a standard value or finding an expert to make the estimate is a logical choice. Analyzing records and searching databases are less likely alternatives at the forecasting stage. Securing estimates from stakeholders is the technique of last resort.

Estimating the program's costs should be an easy step; costs can easily be anticipated on the basis of previous or similar programs, factoring in reasonable assumptions about the program. To achieve a fully loaded cost profile, include all cost categories.

The anticipated intangibles are merely speculation in forecasting but can be reliable indicators of which measures may be influenced in addition to those included in the ROI calculation. At this point, it is assumed that these measures will not be converted to monetary values.

The formula used to calculate the ROI is the same as that used in post-program analysis. The monetary value from the data conversion, minus the estimated program cost, is included as the numerator, and the estimated cost of the program is inserted as the denominator. The projected benefit-cost analysis can be developed along with the ROI.

Steps for Forecasting ROI

Eighteen detailed steps are necessary to develop a credible pre-program ROI forecast, using expert input:

1. *Understand the situation.* Individuals providing input to the forecast and conducting the forecast must understand the present situation very well. Naturally, knowledge of the situation is a major requirement to consider when selecting experts.

2. *Predict the present.* A program is sometimes initiated because a particular business impact measure is not doing well. However, such measures often lag the present situation; they may be based on data that are several months old, especially if they are based on dynamic influences that can change dramatically and quickly. It may be beneficial to estimate the current value of the measure, based on assumptions and current trends. Market share data, for example, are often several months old. Trending market share data and examining other influences driving market share can help organizations understand the current situation. Although this appears to be a lot of work, it is not a new responsibility for most of the experts, who are often concerned about the present situation.

3. *Observe warnings.* Closely tied to predicting the present is making sure that warning signs are observed. Red flags signal that something is going against the measure in question, causing it to go in an undesired direction or otherwise not move as it should. These warning signs often raise concerns that lead to programs; they are early warnings that things may get worse. Consequently, it is important that they be factored into the situation as forecasts are made.

4. *Describe the new process, project, program, or solution.* The program must be completely and clearly described to the experts so that they fully understand the mechanics of what is to be implemented. The description should include the scope of the program, the individuals involved, time factors, and whatever else is necessary to express the magnitude of the program.

5. *Develop specific objectives.* These objectives should mirror the levels of evaluation and should include reaction objectives,

learning objectives, application objectives, and impact objectives. Although these may be difficult to develop, they are developed as part of the up-front analysis described in *ROI Fundamentals*, book one of this series. Objectives provide clear direction toward the program's end. The cascading levels of evaluation represent the anticipated chain of impact that will occur as the program is implemented.

6. *Estimate what participants will think about the program.* In this step, the experts try to understand participants' reactions. Will participants support the program? How will they support it? What may cause participants to become unsupportive? The response is important because a negative reaction can cause a program to fail.

7. *Estimate what participants will learn.* To some extent, every program will involve learning, and the experts must estimate what learning will occur. Using the learning objectives, the experts define what the participants will learn, identifying specific knowledge, skills, and information the participants must acquire or enhance during the program.

8. *Anticipate what participants should accomplish in the program.* Building on the application objectives, the experts identify what will be accomplished as the program is implemented successfully. This step details specific actions, tasks, and processes that will be taken by the participants. Steps 6, 7, and 8 provide important information on participants' anticipated reactions, learning, and application of learning that serves as the basis for the next step: estimating improvement in business impact data.

9. *Estimate the improvement in business impact data.* This is a critical step in that the data generated are needed for the financial forecast. The experts provide an estimate—in either absolute numbers or percentages—of the monetary change in the business impact measure (ΔP). While accuracy is important, it is also important to remember that a forecast is no more than an

estimate based on the best data available at a given time; this is why the next step is included.

10. *Apply the confidence estimate.* Because the estimate given in the previous step is not very accurate, an error adjustment is needed. Therefore, a confidence estimate is placed on the value identified in step 9. The experts are asked to indicate the confidence they have in the data they have provided. The confidence level is expressed as a percentage; 0 indicates "no confidence," and 100 indicates "certainty." The confidence level becomes a discount factor in the analysis.

11. *Convert the business impact data to monetary values.* Using one or more of the methods described in *Data Conversion*, book four in this series, the data are converted to monetary values. One value in particular, designated by the letter *V*, is calculated. If the impact measure represents a desired improvement—for example, in productivity—*V* represents the monetary gain obtained by attaining one more unit of the measure. If the impact measure is one that the organization is trying to reduce—for example, downtime, mistakes, or complaints—*V* is the cost that the organization incurs as a result of one incident. For example, the cost of one instance of voluntary employee turnover may be 1.5 times the employee's annual pay.

12. *Calculate the estimated annual impact of each measure.* The estimated annual impact is the predicted improvement directly related to the program in the year after implementation. In formula form, this value is expressed as follows:

$$\Delta I = (\Delta P \times V) \times 12$$

where

$\Delta I =$ annual change in monetary value

$\Delta P =$ annual change in performance on the impact measure

$V =$ the value of one unit of improvement in the impact measure

If the measure is weekly or monthly, it must be converted to an annual amount. For example, if three lost-time accidents will be prevented each month, the three is multiplied by twelve; the number of accidents that will be prevented annually total thirty-six. If it were three per week and employees worked forty-eight weeks during a year, the value of change in performance would be multiplied by forty-eight for a total of 144 lost-time accidents prevented.

13. *Factor additional years into the analysis for programs that will have a significant useful life beyond the first year.* For these programs, the factor should reflect a diminished benefit in subsequent years. The client or sponsor of the program should provide some indication of the amount of the reduction and the values of performance measures that are desired in the second, third, and successive years. It is important to be conservative by using the smallest numbers possible.

14. *Estimate the fully loaded program cost.* Use all the cost categories described in this book, and denote the value with the letter C when including it in the ROI equation. Include all direct and indirect costs in the calculation.

15. *Calculate the forecast ROI.* Use the total projected benefits and the estimated costs in the standard ROI formula. Calculate the forecast ROI as follows:

$$\text{ROI (\%)} = \frac{\Delta I - C}{C} \times 100$$

16. *Use sensitivity analysis to develop several potential ROI values with different levels of improvement* (ΔP). When more than one measure is changing, the analysis may take the form of a spreadsheet that shows various output scenarios and the subsequent ROI forecasts. Identify the break-even point.

17. *Identify potential intangible benefits.* Anticipate intangible benefits, using input from those most knowledgeable about the situation. Their assumptions will be based on their experience

with similar programs. Remember, intangible benefits are benefits that are not converted to monetary values but that possess value nonetheless.

18. *Communicate the ROI projection and anticipated intangibles with caution.* The target audience must clearly understand that the forecast is based on several assumptions (which should be clearly defined) and that although the values are the best possible estimates, they may include a degree of error.

Following these steps will enable an individual to forecast ROI.

Sources of Expert Input

Several sources of expert input are available for estimating improvement in impact data when a program is implemented. Ideally, experience with similar programs in the organization will inform the estimates made by experts. Experts may include

- Clients or sponsors

- Members of a project team

- Prospective participants

- Subject matter experts

- External experts

- Advocates (individuals who can champion the program)

- Finance and accounting staff

- Analysts (if involved with the program)

- Executives or managers

- Customers

These sources provide an array of possibilities for assistance in estimating the value of an improvement. Because error is part of the process, ask for a confidence measure when using estimates from any source.

With the experts clearly identified, three major steps must be addressed before developing the ROI: input must be gathered from the experts, the data must be converted to monetary values, and costs must be estimated.

Securing Input

First, data must be collected from the individuals whom you have recruited as experts. If the number of individuals is small (for example, if one person from each of the appropriate expert groups is involved), a short interview with each expert may suffice. During interviews, it is critical to avoid bias and to ask clear, succinct questions that are not leading. Questions should be framed in a balanced way in order to capture what may not occur as well as what may occur. If groups are involved, using focus groups may be suitable. For large numbers of people, surveys or questionnaires may be appropriate.

When the groups are diverse and scattered, the Delphi technique may be appropriate. This technique, originally developed by the Rand Corporation in the 1950s, has been used in forecasting and decision making in a variety of disciplines. The Delphi technique was originally devised to help experts achieve better forecasts than they might obtain through traditional group meetings by allowing individuals access to the group without in-person contact. The essential features of a Delphi procedure are anonymity, continual iteration, controlled feedback to participants, and a physical summary of responses. Anonymity is achieved by means of a questionnaire that allows group members to express their opinions and judgments privately. Between all iterations of the questionnaire, the facilitator informs the participants of the opinions of their anonymous colleagues. Typically, this feedback is presented as a simple statistical summary, using mean or median values. The facilitator takes the statistical average in the final round to be the group's judgment (Armstrong, 2001).

In some cases, benchmarking data may be available and can be considered as a source of input for the process of estimating ROI. Previous studies may provide essential input to the process as well. Perhaps an extensive search of databases, using a variety of search engines, will provide useful information that will help in making predictions. The important point is to understand, as much as possible, what may occur as a result of the program.

Conversion to Money

The measures forecast by the experts must be converted to monetary values for one, two, three, or more years, depending on the nature and scope of the program. Standard values are likely to be available for many of these measures. Considering their importance, someone has probably placed monetary values on them. If not, experts are often available to convert the data to monetary values. Otherwise, existing records or databases may be appropriate sources of conversion factors. Another option is to ask stakeholders—perhaps some of the experts listed earlier—to provide the monetary values for the forecast. This step is the only means of showing the money that will be made from the program. *Data Conversion*, book four in this series, covers these techniques in detail.

Estimating Program Costs

Program cost estimates should be based on the most reliable information available and should include the typical categories outlined earlier in this book. The estimates can be based on costs of previous programs. Although the costs are unknown, this task is often relatively easy because of its similarity to budgeting, a process with routine procedures and policies that most practitioners are familiar with. Dividing costs into categories representing the functional processes of the program provides additional insight into program costs. Areas often not given enough attention include analysis, assessment, evaluation, and reporting. If these elements are not properly addressed, much of the value of the program may be missed.

———————

Once the costs and monetary benefits have been estimated, the ROI forecast can be made, using the calculations presented earlier.

Case Study: Retail Merchandise Company—Part A: Pre-Program ROI Forecasting

Considering a case study in which different forecasting issues are explored is instructive. Throughout the rest of this chapter, parts of this case study that are relevant to various sections will be explored.

Situation

Retail Merchandise Company (RMC) is a national chain of 420 stores, located in most major U.S. markets. RMC sells small household items, gifts of all types, electronics, and jewelry, as well as personal accessories. It does not sell clothes or major appliances. RMC executives had been concerned about slow sales growth and were experimenting with several programs designed to boost sales. One concern focused on interaction with customers. Sales associates were not actively involved in the sales process; they usually waited for a customer to make a purchasing decision and then processed the sale. Several store managers had analyzed the situation to determine whether more communication with customers would boost sales. The analysis revealed that the use of very simple techniques to probe for a customer's needs and then guide him or her to a purchase should boost sales in each store.

The senior executives asked the training and development staff to consider implementing a very simple program to teach customer interaction skills to a small group of sales associates. The management team asked the staff to forecast the impact and ROI of the proposed program. If the program's forecast showed an increase in sales and represented a significant payoff for RMC, it would be pilot-tested in a small number of stores.

Proposed Solution

The training and development staff conducted a brief initial needs assessment and identified five simple skills that would need to be covered in the program. Their analysis revealed that the sales associates did not have these skills or were very uncomfortable with using them. The staff selected a program called Interactive Selling Skills that included a significant amount of skill practice. The first part of the program would consist of two days of training, during which the participants would have an opportunity to practice each of the skills with a classmate. After three weeks of on-the-job application of their new skills, the participants would have a final day of training that included a discussion of problems, issues, barriers, and concerns about using the skills. The program, an existing product from an external training supplier, would be taught by the staff of the training supplier for a predetermined facilitation fee. A pre-program forecast was a consideration.

The training and development manager contacted the experts listed in Table 5.1, who provided estimates of the sales increase that would be attributed to the proposed program in three months. Each expert was provided with a description of the program, the skills that would be taught, and the need that it would fill. Each estimate was a best guess based on the person's experience and perspective. Table 5.1 shows their estimates and the calculated ROI for each estimate.

Certain experts have more credibility than others, depending on the target audience perspective. The sales associates don't have a clear understanding of the program. They see no value in the program because they see it as nothing but additional work for them. They may be concerned that customers do not want this additional help and they may also be concerned that this program will mean extra work for them in the future. The vendor sees the most value in the program, but then again, it is the vendor's program. The finance staff is conservative, and the marketing analyst is conservative as well.

Table 5.1. Sales Increase Estimates

Source of Expert Input	Estimated Improvement (Δ)	ROI Forecast
Sales associates	0%	−100%
Department managers	5	−30
Store managers	10	33
Senior executive (sponsor)	15	110
Analyst (needs assessment)	12	95
Vendor (program supplier)	25	350
Marketing analyst	4	−40
Finance staff	2	−80
Benchmarking data	9	22

While the estimates provide the best guess, in collecting these data it is important to also understand the basis on which these individuals arrived at their conclusions. Asking them specifically how they arrived at their estimates would be helpful in assessing their credibility. By adjusting for their confidence in the estimates, a more conservative (and credible) forecast can be developed. In addition, perhaps a credibility ranking for each individual's input from the individual or group who collected the data would be helpful.

Presenting pre-program forecast data to senior mangers presents some challenges due to the variance between estimates. Also pre-program forecasts are often much more generous than the actual ROI of a program. A pre-program forecast should be presented as a matrix, much the way it is shown in Table 5.1.

The break-even point should be calculated to show the management team how much sales need to increase to achieve a break-even scenario.

The person presenting the data (program manager or coordinator) is not included on the list of experts. Although this person might know the potential impact of this program, his or her credibility and potential bias are issues. Also, if the presenter has a recommendation, that will be the number that the group remembers.

ROI Forecast with a Pilot Program

Although the steps presented earlier in this chapter provide a process for estimating the ROI when a pilot program is not conducted, the more favorable approach is to develop a small-scale pilot program and calculate the ROI based on post-program data. This scenario involves the following steps:

1. As in the previous process, develop Level 1, 2, 3, and 4 objectives.

2. Initiate a simple pilot program, without bells and whistles, on a small sample. This strategy keeps the cost extremely low without sacrificing the fundamentals of the program.

3. Fully implement the program with one or more of the typical groups of individuals who can benefit from it. This will require that participants engage in any information sessions as well as apply the information acquired from those sessions.

4. Calculate the ROI, using the ROI model for post-program analysis (the ROI Methodology that is discussed throughout this series).

5. Finally, decide whether to implement the program throughout the organization, given the results of the pilot program.

Post-program evaluation of a pilot program provides much more accurate information on which to base decisions about full implementation of the program. In a pilot program, data can be developed on all six types of measures outlined in this series.

ROI Forecast with Reaction Data

When reaction data include planned applications of the program, these important data can ultimately be used to forecast ROI. By asking how participants plan to use the program and the results that they expect to achieve, more valuable evaluation information

Exhibit 5.1. Important Questions to Ask on Feedback Questionnaires

Planned Improvements

As a result of this program, what specific actions will you attempt as you apply what you have learned?

_____

_____

_____

Please indicate what specific measures, outcomes, or projects will change as a result of your actions.

_____

_____

_____

As a result of the anticipated changes in the measures listed above, please estimate (in monetary values) the benefits to your organization over a period of one year._____

What is the basis of this estimate?

_____

_____

_____

What confidence, expressed as a percentage, can you put in your estimate? (0% = No Confidence; 100% = Certainty)

_____%

_____

can be collected. The questions presented in Exhibit 5.1 illustrate how data are collected with an end-of-program questionnaire. Participants are asked to state specifically how they plan to use the program material and the results that they expect to achieve. They are asked to convert their accomplishments to an annual monetary value and show the basis for the estimate. Participants can moderate their responses with a confidence estimate, which makes the data more credible and allows participants to reflect their uncertainty about the process.

When data are tabulated, the confidence level is multiplied by the annual monetary value, which yields a conservative estimate for use in the data analysis. For example, if a participant estimated that the monetary impact of a program will be $10,000 but is only 50 percent confident, a value of $5,000 is used in the calculations.

To develop a summary of the expected benefits, several steps are taken. First, any data that are incomplete, unusable, extreme, or unrealistic are discarded. This practice follows Guiding Principle 8: "Avoid use of extreme items and unsupported claims when calculating ROI."

Next, an adjustment is made for the confidence estimate, as previously described. Individual data items are then totaled.

Following the confidence adjustment, as an optional exercise, the total value is adjusted again by a factor that reflects the subjectivity of the process and the possibility that participants will not achieve the results they anticipate. In many programs, the participants are very enthusiastic about what they have learned and may be overly optimistic about expected accomplishments. This factor adjusts for participants' overestimation. The adjustment factor can be developed with input from management or established by the staff. In one organization, the benefits are multiplied by 50 percent to develop an even more conservative number to use in the ROI equation.

Finally, the ROI is calculated, using the net program benefits divided by the program costs. This value, in essence, becomes the expected return on investment, after the two adjustments for accuracy and subjectivity.

A word of caution is in order when Level 1 ROI data are used to estimate ROI. These calculations are subjective and may not reflect the extent to which participants will actually apply what they have learned to achieve results. A variety of influences in the work environment can enhance or inhibit participants' attainment of performance goals. Having high expectations at the end of a program is no guarantee that those expectations will be met. Disappointments are documented regularly in programs throughout the world and are reported in research findings (Kaufman, 2002).

While this process is subjective and possibly unreliable, it does have some usefulness. First, if evaluation must stop at this level, this approach provides more insight into the value of a program than data from typical reaction questionnaires. Managers usually find estimated ROI data more useful than a report stating, "40 percent of participants rated the program above average." Unfortunately, a high percentage of evaluations stop at this first level of evaluation. The majority of programs do not enjoy rigorous evaluations at Levels 3 and 4. Reporting Level 1 ROI data is a more useful indication of the potential impact of a program than the alternative of reporting attitudes and feelings about the program.

Second, ROI forecast data can form a basis for comparison of different presentations of the same program. If one version of the program forecasts an ROI of 300 percent, whereas another projects 30 percent, it appears that the first program may have been more effective than the other one. The participants in the first program have more confidence in their planned application of the program material.

Third, collecting data for the ROI estimate brings increased attention to program outcomes. Participants leave the program with an understanding that specific behavior change is expected, and this knowledge produces results for the organization. The issue becomes very clear to participants as they anticipate results and convert them to monetary values. Even if their projected improvement is ignored, the exercise is productive because of the important message that has been sent to participants. It helps to change mindsets about the value, impact, and importance of the program.

Fourth, if a follow-up is planned in order to pinpoint postprogram results, the data collected in the Level 1 evaluation can be very helpful for comparison. For example, in a selling program for Wachovia Bank, the results after the program were compared with the forecast results. Such comparison builds the credibility of a forecasting method. End-of-program data collection also helps participants plan the implementation of what they have learned.

Fifth, the data can be used to secure support for follow-up. For example, most executives, when they see ROI forecast data, will quickly say that they don't believe these data, perhaps with good reason. The best way to see whether the results will materialize is to conduct a follow-up. This is an excellent way to secure support for follow-up when support is absent. Essentially, the data are leveraged to build that support.

The use of Level 1 ROI is increasing; organizations are basing a larger part of their ROI calculations on Level 1 data. Although such estimates may be very subjective, they do add value, particularly when they are part of a comprehensive evaluation system.

Case Study: Retail Merchandise Company—Part B: Level 1 ROI Forecasting

The Retail Merchandise Company implemented a new program called Interactive Selling Skills on a pilot basis in order to improve sales performance. In all, forty-eight sales associates were involved (three groups of sixteen). Sales growth is always a critical issue at RMC and usually commands much management attention. The program focused on initiating simple dialogue with customers, assisting them, and guiding them to a purchase decision. Program participants were expected to improve sales within three months after attending the program. At the end of the three-day program, participants completed a comprehensive reaction questionnaire that asked about specific action items planned as a result of the program and the expected sales increase that could be attributed to the use of skills. In addition, participants were asked to explain the basis for their estimates and place a confidence level on them. The first group of participants provided the data shown in Table 5.2.

After receiving the data, the first step is to analyze the data, using the Guiding Principles as a guide to help determine how to manage

Table 5.2. Data from Participants in Interactive Selling Skills Program

Participant Number	Sales Increase Estimate	Basis	Confidence Level
1	25%	Sales	90%
2	20	2 sales per day	80
3	30	Sales increase	70
4	40	3 sales daily	60
5	30	4 sales each day	95
6	100	More sales	100
7	30	3 more sales	80
8	50	4 sales	75
9	10	1 more sale	30
10	22	2 new sales	80
11	25	Sales	90
12	15	2 sales each day	70
13	0	No increase	60
14	100	Many new sales	95
15	50	Additional sales	50
16	Unlimited	More sales and satisfaction	100

responses. A first step is to look for the error adjustment—have participants adjusted data for confidence? Then toss out extreme or unrealistic data.

On the face of it, these data may not seem very reliable. They came from people who are estimating, perhaps in an optimistic way, the sales increase that they expect to achieve. These participants are excited. They see opportunity and value in the new skills that they have acquired. However, the data can be used in a variety of ways. For example, the process of gathering these data focuses participants on results. It requires that they think more about results and not solely about the learning activity. Also, by gathering these data, the program owner can provide the client with a level of comfort that something will change as a result of the program, a greater level than can be offered from data acquired using a typical Level 1 questionnaire. Finally, a program owner wanting to implement a full-blown ROI study can use these data to pique the interest of the client in hopes of gaining funding necessary to conduct the study, as the following material explains.

ROI Forecast with Learning Data

Testing for changes in skills and knowledge is a very common technique for evaluating learning in programs (Level 2 evaluation). In many situations, participants are required to demonstrate their knowledge or skills at the end of a program, and their performance is expressed as a numerical value. When this type of test is developed and used, it must be reliable and valid. A reliable test is one that is stable over time, yielding consistent results. A valid test is one that measures what it purports to measure. A test should reflect the content of the program, and successful mastery of program content should be related to improved job performance. As a result, there should be a strong relationship between test scores and subsequent on-the-job performance. The strength of this relationship, expressed as a correlation coefficient, is a measure of test validity. Figure 5.3 illustrates a perfect correlation between test scores and job performance.

Figure 5.3. Relationship Between Test Scores and Job Performance

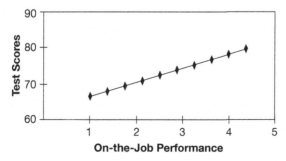

This testing situation provides an excellent opportunity for an ROI calculation with Level 2 data. If there is a statistically significant relationship between test scores and on-the-job performance and the performance can be converted to monetary units, then it is possible to use test scores to estimate the ROI from the program, using the following steps:

- Ensure that the program content reflects the desired on-the-job performance.

- Develop an end-of-program test that reflects program content.

- Establish a statistical relationship between the test data and the output performance of participants.

- Predict performance levels of each participant, using their test scores.

- Convert the performance data to monetary values.

- Compare the net predicted value of the program with program costs.

Case Study: Retail Merchandise Company—Part C: Level 2 ROI Forecasting

When RMC implemented the Interactive Selling Skills program, the program coordinator developed a test in order to predict sales performance based on participants' mastery of the knowledge and skills taught in the program. At the end of the program, participants took the comprehensive test. As part of the test, participants analyzed customer service and sales situations and decided on specific actions. To validate the test, RMC calculated the correlations between test scores and associates' sales performance. The correlation was strong and statistically significant, enabling the program coordinators to use test scores to predict the sales increase for each

Figure 5.4. Correlation Between RMC Test Scores and On-the-Job Sales Increases

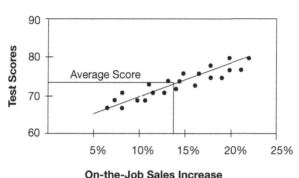

On-the-Job Sales Increase

participant. As a quick way of calculating the estimated return from a program, RMC estimates the output level for each participant, converts the output data to monetary values, and then combines them in order to calculate the estimated ROI. Figure 5.4 shows the correlation.

For the first group of forty-eight participants, the average score on the post-program test was 74, predicting an average sales increase of 14 percent. The average sales per week per associate at the beginning of the program was $9,698. The profit margin was 2 percent, and the cost of the program was $687 per person. A forty-eight-week annual work period was considered.

The ROI is forecast as follows: a 14% sales increase on $9,698 amounts to $1,357. A profit margin of 2 percent means that $27.14 is the profit on the sales increase. However, forty-eight people were involved in the program, so the average profit should be multiplied by forty-eight. Also, the sales measure is a weekly figure, so it should be multiplied by forty-eight weeks in order to yield an annual figure. So the total monetary value is $27.14 × 48 × 48, which equals $62,530. This is the total monetary value of the predicted performance improvement. When this is divided by the cost of the program, or $32,976 ($687 × 48), the BCR is 1:1.9. The forecast predicts that for every dollar invested, $1.90 in benefits will be returned. This translates into a forecast ROI of 90 percent.

This number may not be reliable because it is based on history and does not necessarily indicate what will occur in the future. However, it does provide an indicator of potential program success. This sort of information is useful. In reality, testing relationships such as the one used here may not be known.

Cautions

Again, when end-of-program questionnaires are used, some cautions are in order. The final number is a forecast of the ROI and not the actual value. Although participants acquired skills and knowledge from the program, there is no guarantee that they will apply the techniques and processes successfully and that the desired results will be achieved. This process assumes that the current group of participants has the same relationship to output performance as previous groups. It ignores a variety of environmental influences, which could alter the situation entirely. Finally, the process requires calculating the initial correlation coefficient, which would be difficult to do for most tests.

Advantages

Although this approach develops an estimate based on historical relationships, it can be useful in a comprehensive evaluation strategy because it has several advantages. First, if post-program evaluations (Level 4) are not planned, this process will yield more information about the projected value of the program than would be obtained from raw test scores. This process yields an expected ROI based on the historical relationships involved. Second, because the process develops individual ROI measurements and communicates them to participants, it has the potential to reinforce desired behaviors. It communicates to participants that increased sales and market share are expected as a result of their application of what they learned in the program. Third, this process is likely to have considerable credibility with management and may preclude expensive follow-ups and post-program monitoring. If the relationship on which it is based is statistically sound, the estimate should have credibility with the target audience.

ROI Forecast with Application Data

In almost every program, participants are expected to change their on-the-job behaviors by applying the materials or implementing the program. On-the-job application is critical to program success. Although use of the targeted skills on the job is no guarantee that results will follow, it is an underlying assumption of most programs that if the knowledge and skills are applied, then results will follow. Some of the most prestigious learning organizations, such as Motorola University, base their ultimate evaluation on this assumption. A few organizations take this process a step further by measuring the value of on-the-job behavior change and calculating the ROI. In these situations, estimates are taken from individual participants, their supervisors, the management group, or experts in the field. This process, then, is a forecast of impact, based on changes in behavior on the job immediately after the program. The following steps are used to evaluate the ROI:

1. Specify competencies required in the target job.

2. Indicate what percentage of the job consists of the competencies covered in the program.

3. Determine the monetary value of competencies, using the values of salaries and employee benefits of the participants.

4. Compute the worth of pre-program and post-program skill levels.

5. Subtract post-program values from pre-program values.

6. Compare the net added benefits with the program costs.

This process is described in Chapter Three, where it is called *utility analysis*. It attempts to place a value on the improvement of an individual. Utility analysis examines the behavior change and assigns monetary value based on the salary of the individual; however, it ignores the consequences of the improvement (that is, business impact). Utility analysis is referred to as a Level 3 ROI forecast because it converts changes in behavior to monetary values, using the salaries of the participants as a base.

Case Study: Retail Merchandise Company—Part D: Level 3 ROI Forecasting

RMC implemented the Interactive Selling Skills program, which focused on five basic competencies:

- Identifying customers' needs

- Listening and reacting to customers

- Profiling the user of the product in the electronics department

- Providing excellent customer service

- Recommending specific products

The managers of the sales associates indicated that these five competencies accounted for 55 percent of the sales associate job. In the group that was evaluated, the average annual salary (plus benefits) was $17,332. Multiplying this figure by the amount of job success accounted for by the five competencies (55 percent) yielded a dollar value of $9,533 per participant. If a person were to perform successfully in these competencies for one year, the value to RMC would be $9,533.

Managers rated the associates' skills on each of the competencies on a scale of 1 to 10 before the program was conducted. The average level of skills required to be successful was determined to be 6.32. The average skill rating prior to the program was 4.12, which represented 65 percent of the 6.32. (That is, participants were performing at 65 percent of the level required to be successful in the competencies.) After the program, the skill rating was 6.24, 99 percent of the level needed to be successful.

Dollar values were assigned to the skill levels, based on the participants' salaries. Performance at the required level was worth $9,533. Thus, when they were at a proficiency level of 65 percent, the sales associates were performing at a contribution value of $6,196. Six weeks after the program, the proficiency level of the sales associates reached 99 percent, representing a contribution of $9,438. The difference in these values ($3,242) represented the gain per participant attributable to the program. The program cost $687 per participant.

The BCR is

$$\text{BCR} = \frac{\$3,242}{\$687} = 4.72$$

For every dollar invested, $4.72 is returned. This translates into a 372 percent ROI. This figure is very high.

The ROI figure lacks some credibility because it does not reflect what participants actually do with the skills. Also, the competencies are not available for analysis. However, this approach could be an important alternative for programs that are difficult to forecast because impact data are not readily available.

This program would be best evaluated at Level 4, using actual data collected at the impact level after program implementation. However, for leadership programs in which the impact data may take a variety of forms, this may be a valid approach.

Advantages

Although this process is subjective, it has several useful advantages. First, if there are no plans to track the measurable business impact of a program (Level 4), this approach represents a credible substitute. In many programs—particularly skill-building and competency programs—identifying tangible changes on the job may be difficult. As a result, alternative approaches to determining the worth of a program are needed. Second, this method (utility analysis) has been developed in the literature, so there are several models that can be used. Third, this approach results in data that are usually credible with the top management group if they understand how they were developed and the assumptions behind them. An important point is that the data on the changes in competence level came from the managers, who rated their direct reports, which increases the level of credibility. In this case, the numbers were large enough to make the process statistically significant.

Guidelines for Forecasting

Given the many different time frames for forecasting that are outlined in this chapter, a few guidelines may help you sort through the forecasting possibilities within your organization. These guidelines are based on experience in forecasting a variety of programs (Bowers, 1997).

If You Must Forecast, Forecast Frequently

Forecasting is a process that is both an art and a science, and it needs to be pursued regularly in order to build comfort, experience, and history with the process. Also, those who use the data need to see forecasts frequently in order to integrate forecasting into the evaluation mix.

Consider Forecasting an Essential Evaluation Tool

The first chapter of this book ended with a list of reasons why forecasting ROI is important. The concept is growing in use, and ROI forecasts are being demanded by many organizations. ROI forecasting can be an effective and useful tool when used properly and employed in conjunction with other types of evaluation data. Some organizations have targets for the use of forecasting (for example, if a program exceeds a certain cost, a pre-program forecast will be required). Other organizations target a certain number of programs for a forecast based on reaction data and use the forecasts in the manner described in this chapter. Still other organizations specify some low-level targets for forecasting at Levels 2 and 3. The important point is that you plan for the forecasts and let them be a part of the evaluation mix that is used regularly.

Forecast Different Types of Data

Although most of this chapter focuses on how to develop a forecast using the standard ROI formula, it is helpful to forecast other types of data. A usable, helpful forecast will include predictions about reaction and planned action, the extent of learning, and the extent of application and implementation. Also, the intangible data can be forecast. These types of data are important in anticipating movements and shifts, based on the planned program. Forecasting many types of data is not only helpful in developing the overall forecast but important in understanding the total anticipated impact of the program.

Secure Input from Those Who Know the Process Best

As forecasts are developed, it is essential to gather input from the individuals who best understand the dynamics of the workplace and the measures being influenced by the program. Sometimes, program participants or their immediate managers are the best source. In other situations, a variety of analysts are aware of the major influences in the workplace and the dynamics of those changes. Go to the experts. It will increase the accuracy of your forecast as well as the credibility of the final results.

Understand That Long-Term Forecasts Will Usually Be Inaccurate

Forecasting works much better in a short time frame. For most short-term scenarios, a better grasp of the influences that might drive the measure is possible. When you are working on a long-term basis, a variety of unforeseen new influences can enter the process and drastically change the impact measures. If a long-term forecast is needed, it should be updated regularly as part of a continuously improving process.

Expect Forecasts to Be Biased

Forecasts consist of data coming from those who have an interest in the issue. Some will want the forecast to be optimistic; others will have a pessimistic view. Almost all input is biased in one way or another. Every attempt should be made to minimize the bias, adjust for the bias, and adjust for the uncertainty in the process. Still, your audience will need to recognize that despite your best efforts to eliminate bias, a forecast is a biased prediction.

Commit to the Hard Work of Serious Forecasting

The value of forecasting often depends on the amount of effort put into the process. High-stakes programs need to take a serious approach, collecting all possible data, examining different scenarios, and making the best prediction possible. In these situations, mathematical tools can be valuable aids.

Routinely Review the Success of Forecasting

As forecasts are made, it is imperative that you revisit the forecast with actual post-program data to check the accuracy and the success of the forecast. Performing such reviews on a regular basis aids in the continuous improvement of forecasting processes. Sources may prove to be more credible or less credible, and specific inputs may be more biased or less biased. Some analyses may be more appropriate than others. Constant improvement of the methods and approaches for forecasting within the organization is critical to success.

Be Aware That Assumptions Are the Most Serious Errors in Forecasting

Of all the variables that enter into the forecasting process, the ones with the greatest potential for error are the assumptions made by the individual providing the forecast. Assumptions must be clearly understood and communicated. When multiple inputs are involved, each forecaster should use the same set of assumptions, if possible.

Keep in Mind That Decision Making Is the Purpose of Forecasting

The most important use of forecasting is providing information and input for decision makers. Forecasting is a tool for those who are trying to make decisions about a program. It is not a process for maximizing the output or minimizing any particular variable. It is not a process for dramatically changing the way in which programs are implemented. It is a process for providing data for decisions; that's the greatest utility of forecasting.

Final Thoughts

This chapter illustrates that ROI forecasts can be developed at different points in the life cycle of a program. Although most practitioners and researchers use application and impact data for ROI calculations, there are situations in which Level 3 and Level 4 data are not available or evaluations at those levels are not planned or attempted. ROI forecasts that are developed before a program is implemented can be useful to management and staff, focusing attention on the potential economic impact of a program. Forecasts based on reaction data or learning data are also possible.

Be aware that ROI forecasts may result in a false sense of accuracy. On one hand, as would be expected, pre-program ROI forecasts are the lowest in credibility and accuracy but have the advantage of being inexpensive and relatively easy to conduct. On the other hand, ROI forecasts using Level 3 data are highest in credibility and accuracy but are more expensive and difficult to develop.

Although ROI calculations based on impact (Level 4) data are preferred, ROI forecasts based on other types of data are an important part of a comprehensive and systematic evaluation process. Integrating forecasts into the evaluation routine usually means that targets for different types of ROI forecasts should be established.

References

Armstrong, S. *Principles of Forecasting: A Handbook for Researchers and Practitioners.* Boston: Kluwer, 2001.

Bowers, D. *Forecasting for Control and Profit.* Menlo Park, Calif.: Crisp Publications, 1997.

Kaufman, R. "Resolving the (Often-Deserved) Attacks on Training." *Performance Improvement*, 2002, 41(6), pp. 5–6.

Index

About the Authors

Jack J. Phillips, Ph.D., a world-renowned expert on accountability, measurement, and evaluation, provides consulting services for Fortune 500 companies and major global organizations. The author or editor of more than fifty books, Phillips conducts workshops and makes conference presentations throughout the world.

His expertise in measurement and evaluation is based on more than twenty-seven years of corporate experience in the aerospace, textile, metals, construction materials, and banking industries. Phillips has served as training and development manager at two Fortune 500 firms, as senior human resources officer at two firms, as president of a regional bank, and as management professor at a major state university. This background led Phillips to develop the ROI Methodology, a revolutionary process that provides bottom-line figures and accountability for all types of learning, performance improvement, human resources, technology, and public policy programs.

Phillips regularly consults with clients in manufacturing, service, and government organizations in forty-four countries in North and South America, Europe, Africa, Australia, and Asia.

Books most recently authored by Phillips include *Show Me the Money: How to Determine ROI in People, Projects, and Programs* (Berrett-Koehler, 2007); *The Value of Learning* (Pfeiffer, 2007); *How to Build a Successful Consulting Practice* (McGraw-Hill,

2006); *Investing in Your Company's Human Capital: Strategies to Avoid Spending Too Much or Too Little* (Amacom, 2005); *Proving the Value of HR: How and Why to Measure ROI* (Society for Human Resource Management, 2005); *The Leadership Scorecard* (Butterworth-Heinemann, 2004); *Managing Employee Retention* (Butterworth-Heinemann, 2003); *Return on Investment in Training and Performance Improvement Programs*, 2nd edition (Butterworth-Heinemann, 2003); *The Project Management Scorecard* (Butterworth-Heinemann, 2002); *How to Measure Training Results* (McGraw-Hill, 2002); *The Human Resources Scorecard: Measuring the Return on Investment* (Butterworth-Heinemann, 2001); *The Consultant's Scorecard* (McGraw-Hill, 2000); and *Performance Analysis and Consulting* (ASTD, 2000). Phillips served as series editor for the In Action casebook series of the American Society for Training and Development (ASTD), an ambitious publishing project featuring thirty titles. He currently serves as series editor for Butterworth-Heinemann's Improving Human Performance series and for Pfeiffer's new Measurement and Evaluation series.

Phillips has received several awards for his books and his work. The Society for Human Resource Management presented him with an award for one of his books and honored a Phillips ROI study with its highest award for creativity. ASTD gave him its highest award, Distinguished Contribution to Workplace Learning and Development. *Meeting News* named Phillips one of the twenty-five most influential people in the meetings and events industry, based on his work on ROI within the industry.

Phillips holds undergraduate degrees in electrical engineering, physics, and mathematics; a master's degree in decision sciences from Georgia State University; and a Ph.D. degree in human resources management from the University of Alabama.

Jack Phillips has served on the boards of several private businesses—including two NASDAQ companies—and several associations, including ASTD, and nonprofit organizations. He is chairman of the ROI Institute, Inc., and can be reached at (205) 678-8101, or by e-mail at jack@roiinstitute.net.

Lizette Zúñiga, Ph.D., is an independent senior consultant with ROI Institute. With more than fifteen years of professional experience, she has expertise in leadership and team development, conflict resolution, diversity training, organizational culture assessment, merger integration, strategic planning, program evaluation, ROI, survey design, and needs assessment.

Zúñiga has served as both an internal and an external consultant for Fortune 500 companies. Formerly with First Data Corporation, she led the corporate university's team in assessment and measurement efforts. She executed a university dashboard, linking strategic business objectives to organizational development initiatives as well as critical success factors and key measures. She executed impact studies showing the value of learning and development efforts. In her current capacity as a performance consultant, she assists organizations by conducting various types of assessments and surveys, including organizational culture assessment, needs assessment, and leadership competency assessment. She also assesses the business impact of organizational development interventions and facilitates leadership and team development activities. The impact studies she has conducted address such areas as e-learning, leadership development, sales performance, organizational change interventions, mergers and acquisitions, call center simulation, career development, and use of technology.

Zúñiga's academic contribution is extensive. She has served as an adjunct professor for a major university, teaching adult learning theory and practice and presentation skills, and she currently facilitates a three-day certification course in measuring and evaluating learning and a two-day certification course in ROI for ASTD. She also serves as an online instructor for the University Alliance ROI certification course and is an associate with the ROI Institute. She holds a master's degree in psychology with a concentration in cross-cultural psychology and psychometry from Georgia State University and a Ph.D. degree in leadership and human resource development (HRD) from Barry University. She is certified in Myers-Briggs typology and in ROI evaluation. She has also contributed to the HRD literature by publishing several articles on ROI and program evaluation.

Pfeiffer Publications Guide

This guide is designed to familiarize you with the various types of Pfeiffer publications. The formats section describes the various types of products that we publish; the methodologies section describes the many different ways that content might be provided within a product. We also provide a list of the topic areas in which we publish.

FORMATS

In addition to its extensive book-publishing program, Pfeiffer offers content in an array of formats, from fieldbooks for the practitioner to complete, ready-to-use training packages that support group learning.

FIELDBOOK Designed to provide information and guidance to practitioners in the midst of action. Most fieldbooks are companions to another, sometimes earlier, work, from which its ideas are derived; the fieldbook makes practical what was theoretical in the original text. Fieldbooks can certainly be read from cover to cover. More likely, though, you'll find yourself bouncing around following a particular theme, or dipping in as the mood, and the situation, dictate.

HANDBOOK A contributed volume of work on a single topic, comprising an eclectic mix of ideas, case studies, and best practices sourced by practitioners and experts in the field.

An editor or team of editors usually is appointed to seek out contributors and to evaluate content for relevance to the topic. Think of a handbook not as a ready-to-eat meal, but as a cookbook of ingredients that enables you to create the most fitting experience for the occasion.

RESOURCE Materials designed to support group learning. They come in many forms: a complete, ready-to-use exercise (such as a game); a comprehensive resource on one topic (such as conflict management) containing a variety of methods and approaches; or a collection of like-minded activities (such as icebreakers) on multiple subjects and situations.

TRAINING PACKAGE An entire, ready-to-use learning program that focuses on a particular topic or skill. All packages comprise a guide for the facilitator/trainer and a workbook for the participants. Some packages are supported with additional media—such as video—or learning aids, instruments, or other devices to help participants understand concepts or practice and develop skills.

- *Facilitator/trainer's guide* Contains an introduction to the program, advice on how to organize and facilitate the learning event, and step-by-step instructor notes. The guide also contains copies of presentation materials—handouts, presentations, and overhead designs, for example—used in the program.

- *Participant's workbook* Contains exercises and reading materials that support the learning goal and serves as a valuable reference and support guide for participants in the weeks and months that follow the learning event. Typically, each participant will require his or her own workbook.

ELECTRONIC CD-ROMs and web-based products transform static Pfeiffer content into dynamic, interactive experiences. Designed to take advantage of the searchability, automation, and ease-of-use that technology provides, our e-products bring convenience and immediate accessibility to your workspace.

METHODOLOGIES

CASE STUDY A presentation, in narrative form, of an actual event that has occurred inside an organization. Case studies are not prescriptive, nor are they used to prove a point; they are designed to develop critical analysis and decision-making skills. A case study has a specific time frame, specifies a sequence of events, is narrative in structure, and contains a plot structure—an issue (what should be/have been done?). Use case studies when the goal is to enable participants to apply previously learned theories to the circumstances in the case, decide what is pertinent, identify the real issues, decide what should have been done, and develop a plan of action.

ENERGIZER A short activity that develops readiness for the next session or learning event. Energizers are most commonly used after a break or lunch to stimulate or refocus the group. Many involve some form of physical activity, so they are a useful way to counter post-lunch lethargy. Other uses include transitioning from one topic to another, where "mental" distancing is important.

EXPERIENTIAL LEARNING ACTIVITY (ELA) A facilitator-led intervention that moves participants through the learning cycle from experience to application (also known as a Structured Experience). ELAs are carefully thought-out designs in which there is a definite learning purpose and intended outcome. Each step—everything that participants do during the activity—facilitates the accomplishment of the stated goal. Each ELA includes complete instructions for facilitating the intervention and a clear statement of goals, suggested group size and timing, materials required, an explanation of the process, and, where appropriate, possible variations to the activity. (For more detail on Experiential Learning Activities, see the Introduction to the *Reference Guide to Handbooks and Annuals*, 1999 edition, Pfeiffer, San Francisco.)

GAME A group activity that has the purpose of fostering team spirit and togetherness in addition to the achievement of a pre-stated goal. Usually contrived—undertaking a desert expedition, for example—this type of learning method offers an engaging means for participants to demonstrate and practice business and interpersonal skills. Games are effective for team building and personal development mainly because the goal is subordinate to the process—the means through which participants reach decisions, collaborate, communicate, and generate trust and understanding. Games often engage teams in "friendly" competition.

ICEBREAKER A (usually) short activity designed to help participants overcome initial anxiety in a training session and/or to acquaint the participants with one another. An icebreaker can be a fun activity or can be tied to specific topics or training goals. While a useful tool in itself, the icebreaker comes into its own in situations where tension or resistance exists within a group.

INSTRUMENT A device used to assess, appraise, evaluate, describe, classify, and summarize various aspects of human behavior. The term used to describe an instrument depends primarily on its format and purpose. These terms include survey, questionnaire, inventory, diagnostic, survey, and poll. Some uses of instruments include providing instrumental feedback to group members, studying here-and-now processes or functioning within a group, manipulating group composition, and evaluating outcomes of training and other interventions.

Instruments are popular in the training and HR field because, in general, more growth can occur if an individual is provided with a method for focusing specifically on his or her own behavior. Instruments also are used to obtain information that will serve as a basis for change and to assist in workforce planning efforts.

Paper-and-pencil tests still dominate the instrument landscape with a typical package comprising a facilitator's guide, which offers advice on administering the instrument and interpreting the collected data, and an initial set of instruments. Additional instruments are available separately. Pfeiffer, though, is investing heavily in e-instruments. Electronic instrumentation provides effortless distribution and, for larger groups particularly, offers advantages over paper-and-pencil tests in the time it takes to analyze data and provide feedback.

LECTURETTE A short talk that provides an explanation of a principle, model, or process that is pertinent to the participants' current learning needs. A lecturette is intended to establish a common language bond between the trainer and the participants by providing a mutual frame of reference. Use a lecturette as an introduction to a group activity or event, as an interjection during an event, or as a handout.

MODEL A graphic depiction of a system or process and the relationship among its elements. Models provide a frame of reference and something more tangible, and more easily remembered, than a verbal explanation. They also give participants something to "go on," enabling them to track their own progress as they experience the dynamics, processes, and relationships being depicted in the model.

ROLE PLAY A technique in which people assume a role in a situation/ scenario: a customer service rep in an angry-customer exchange, for example. The way in which the role is approached is then discussed and feedback is offered. The role play is often repeated using a different approach and/or incorporating changes made based on feedback received. In other words, role playing is a spontaneous interaction involving realistic behavior under artificial (and safe) conditions.

SIMULATION A methodology for understanding the interrelationships among components of a system or process. Simulations differ from games in that they test or use a model that depicts or mirrors some aspect of reality in form, if not necessarily in content. Learning occurs by studying the effects of change on one or more factors of the model. Simulations are commonly used to test hypotheses about what happens in a system—often referred to as "what if?" analysis—or to examine best-case/worst-case scenarios.

THEORY A presentation of an idea from a conjectural perspective. Theories are useful because they encourage us to examine behavior and phenomena through a different lens.

TOPICS

The twin goals of providing effective and practical solutions for workforce training and organization development and meeting the educational needs of training and human resource professionals shape Pfeiffer's publishing program. Core topics include the following:

Leadership & Management

Communication & Presentation

Coaching & Mentoring

Training & Development

E-Learning

Teams & Collaboration

OD & Strategic Planning

Human Resources

Consulting

What will you find on pfeiffer.com?

- The best in workplace performance solutions for training and HR professionals

- Downloadable training tools, exercises, and content

- Web-exclusive offers

- Training tips, articles, and news

- Seamless on-line ordering

- Author guidelines, information on becoming a Pfeiffer Affiliate, and much more

Discover more at www.pfeiffer.com

Measurement and Evaluation Series

Series Editors
Patricia Pulliam Phillips, Ph.D., and Jack J. Phillips, Ph.D.

A six-book set that provides a step-by-step system for planning, measuring, calculating, and communicating evaluation and Return-on-Investment for training and development, featuring:

- Detailed templates
- Complete plans
- Ready-to-use tools
- Real-world case examples

The M&E Series features:

1. *ROI Fundamentals: Why and When to Measure ROI*
   (978-0-7879-8716-9)
2. *Data Collection: Planning For and Collecting All Types of Data*
   (978-0-7879-8718-3)
3. *Isolation of Results: Defining the Impact of the Program*
   (978-0-7879-8719-0)
4. *Data Conversion: Calculating the Monetary Benefits*
   (978-0-7879-8720-6)
5. *Costs and ROI: Evaluating at the Ultimate Level*
   (978-0-7879-8721-3)
6. *Communication and Implementation: Sustaining the Practice*
   (978-0-7879-8722-0)

Plus, the *ROI in Action Casebook* (978-0-7879-8717-6) covers all the major workplace learning and performance applications, including Leadership Development, Sales Training, Performance Improvement, Technical Skills Training, Information Technology Training, Orientation and OJT, and Supervisor Training.

The **ROI Methodology** is a comprehensive measurement and evaluation process that collects six types of measures: Reaction, Satisfaction, and Planned Action; Learning; Application and Implementation; Business Impact; Return on Investment; and Intangible Measures. The process provides a step-by-step system for evaluation and planning, data collection, data analysis, and reporting. It is appropriate for the measurement and evaluation of *all* kinds of performance improvement programs and activities, including training and development, learning, human resources, coaching, meetings and events, consulting, and project management.

Special Offer from the ROI Institute

Send for your own ROI Process Model, an indispensable tool for implementing and presenting ROI in your organization. The ROI Institute is offering an exclusive gift to readers of The Measurement and Evaluation Series. This 11"× 25" multicolor foldout shows the ROI Methodology flow model and the key issues surrounding the implementation of the ROI Methodology. This easy-to-understand overview of the ROI Methodology has proven invaluable to countless professionals when implementing the ROI Methodology. Please return this page or e-mail your information to the address below to receive your free foldout (a $6.00 value). Please check your area(s) of interest in ROI.

Please send me the ROI Process Model described in the book. I am interested in learning more about the following ROI materials and services:

☐ Workshops and briefing on ROI   ☐ ROI consulting services
☐ Books and support materials on ROI   ☐ ROI Network information
☐ Certification in the ROI Methodology   ☐ ROI benchmarking
☐ ROI software   ☐ ROI research

Name _____

Title _____

Organization _____

Address _____

Phone _____

E-mail Address _____

Functional area of interest:

☐ Learning and Development/Performance Improvement
☐ Human Resources/Human Capital
☐ Public Relations/Community Affairs/Government Relations
☐ Consulting
☐ Sales/Marketing
☐ Technology/IT Systems
☐ Project Management Solutions
☐ Quality/Six Sigma
☐ Operations/Methods/Engineering
☐ Research and Development/Innovations
☐ Finance/Compliance
☐ Logistics/Distribution/Supply Chain
☐ Public Policy Initiatives
☐ Social Programs
☐ Other (Please Specify) _____

Organizational Level

☐ executive   ☐ management   ☐ consultant   ☐ specialist
☐ student   ☐ evaluator   ☐ researcher

Return this form or contact   The ROI Institute
                                      P.O. Box 380637
                                      Birmingham, AL 35238-0637

Or e-mail information to info@roiinstitute.net
Please allow four to six weeks for delivery.

Printed in the United States
By Bookmasters